Observing Gabb

CW00816176

Observing Gabby

Child Development and Learning 0–7 years

CATH ARNOLD

 Open University Press

Open University Press
McGraw Hill
8th Floor, 338 Euston Road
London
England
NW1 3BH

email: enquiries@openup.co.uk
world wide web: www.openup.co.uk

First edition published 2021

A catalogue record of this book is available from the British Library

ISBN-13: 9780335249978
ISBN-10: 0335249973
eISBN: 9780335249985

Library of Congress Cataloging-in-Publication Data
CIP data applied for

Typeset by Transforma Pvt. Ltd., Chennai, India

Fictitious names of companies, products, people, characters and/or data
that may be used herein (in case studies or in examples) are not intended
to represent any real individual, company, product or event.

Printed in Great Britain by Bell and Bain Ltd, Glasgow

Praise page

Research on children displays unfortunate gaps. Most studies select narrow age-groups, such as "infancy" or "preschoolers", and specific aspects of development. Demands for credibility in research findings favour large samples and distrust of studies that focus on just one child. Observing Gabby demonstrates the value of studying individual children, and of the special perspectives that a grandparent can provide. By illuminating her observations with accessible and reflective accounts of other early years research, Arnold offers a unique portrait, free of judgment and admonition, that will be indispensable reading for parents and carers as well as for academics and students.

*Cary Bazalgette Independent researcher on children
and moving-image media; Honorary Research Fellow,
UCL Institute of Education, UK*

Cath Arnold follows in the footsteps of the empiricist Jean Piaget and practitioners like Vivian Gussin Paley with her latest observational-based book. This carefully structured text will be helpful for anyone teaching or studying child development particularly with the addition of video materials to view alongside the book. Cath links her close observations to theory throughout demonstrating clearly for practitioners who wish to develop their skills of analysis. The links to the Intent/Implementation and Impact at the end of each chapter will support the requirements for Ofsted but more importantly for the enhancement of pedagogy. Throughout the observations, the reader will gain a sense of Gabby as a developing person from birth to seven.

*Mary Briggs FRSA, CMathTeach, APECS, SFHEA,
FCCT, Principal Lecturer and Programme Lead
for Childhood and Education (ECS and Ed Studies),
Oxford Brookes University, UK*

Attending to the domestic minutiae and rhythms of a baby's world, Cath documents her grandchild's life as it expands outwards into the community and early schooling. Rather than seeking to uncover universal truths of child psychology, she offers insights into the art of noticing as a subjective and responsive practice. Child development theories are accessibly woven into this fine-grained pedagogy of shared attention. Cath's project democratises a history of child observation (including Darwin and Piaget), and beautifully demonstrates how observation itself is an act of care that actively participates in the unfolding relationship between Gabby and her family.

Dr Christina MacRae, Manchester Metropolitan University

This rich account of Gabby's early childhood development takes the reader on an inspiring journey. Cath Arnold's insightful analysis of her observations places theoretical perspectives on child development in the context of real life events. A fascinating read for early childhood students and practitioners.

Shirley Allen, School of Health and Education,
Middlesex University

Dr Cath Arnold has produced a wonderful case study of her granddaughter Gabby, documenting Gabby's developmental journey through the first seven years. A delight to read, this book draws on observations from her grandmother and other members of Gabby's family to illustrate Dr Arnold's thinking. She weaves sometimes complicated theory into Gabby's story, making it wonderfully accessible to both practitioners and parents alike. I would heartily recommend this book to any early years practitioner, who wants to better understand child development, improve the quality of their child observations and to develop their skill in linking the two seamlessly.

Andrea Layzell, Project Lead and Tutor,
Bradford Birth to 19 Teaching School Alliance

Contents

List of Video Clips to accompany text online

A few video clips for each year of Gabby's life from 0-7 years are on offer on the website accompanying this book. I have tried to offer at least one clip of around 5 minutes duration for each year, as I have found that to be a good length for analysis. In addition, shorter clips are offered sometimes showing similar play and sometimes contrasting play. Some are analysed in the text and others offer additional material.

https://www.mheducation.co.uk/professionals/open-university-press/olc/observing-gabby

No.	Age Range	Duration	Description	Age in yrs, mnths and days
1.1	0-1	5m 12s	Pegs and Bowl	8m 9d
1.2	0-1	1m 2s	Gabby and IPhone	7m 2d
1.3	0-1	52s	Gabby with pegs and upturned bowl	7m 19d
1.4	0-1	1m 37s	Gabby talking to Teddy	7m 25d
1.5	0-1	23s	Saying Teddy	7m 25d
1.6	0-1	3m 46s	Gabby and scarf	9m 3d
1.7	0-1	4m 3s	Gabby with camera bag and remote	11m 23d
2.1	1-2	3m 13s	Gabby with base of dish 'chuffed'	17m 29d
2.2	1-2	5m 46s	Gabby with Os and Xs	17m 29d
2.3	1-2	2m 31s	Gabby switching lamp	17m 29d
2.4	1-2	4m 10s	Gabby drawing	18m
2.5	1-2	30s	Gabby switching nightlight	19m 2d
2.6	1-2	1m 5s	Gabby in Nicole's slippers	19m 2d
2.7	1-2	3m 10s	Gabby practising fastening seatbelt	18-20m
2.8	1-2	41s	Gabby with scarf for Teddy	20m 2d
2.9	1-2	1m 12s	Gabby and scarf	20m 15d
2.10	1-2	5m 13s	Gabby drawing	22m 4d

No.	Age Range	Duration	Description	Age in yrs, mnths and days
2.11	1-2	4m 5s	Gabby wrapping baby and peep-bo	22m 27d
3.1	2-3	5m 6s	Colours, pens and books	2y 3m 22d
3.2	2-3	1m 13s	Golf ball and slide	2y 2d
3.3	2-3	57s	Gabby jumping	2y 2m 7d
3.4	2-3	8s	At Mini Mischiefs	2y 4m
3.5	2-3	40s	Rolling duck down slide	2y 8m
3.6	2-3	1m 36s	Gabby practising cutting	2y 10m 3d
4.1	3-4	5m 54s	Pretending to write names of people	3y 1m 10d
4.2	3-4	1m 23s	Playing with sensori circles	3y 1m 10d
4.3	3-4	1m 24s	Rotating "really fast"	3y 2m
4.4	3-4	3m	Painting and feeling texture of paint	
5.1	4-5 (1)	29s	Playing with yo yo	4y 10m 9d
5.2	4-5 (2)	16s	Playing with yo yo	4y 10m 9d
5.3	4-5 (3)	1m 16s	Playing with yo yo	4y 10m 9d
5.4	4-5	2m 7s	Writing and sounding words	4y 5m 6d
5.5	4-5	1m 23s	Tricking Mummy (near Xmas)	4y 6m 5d
5.6	4-5	15s	Making a line of books	4y 6m 28d
5.7	4-5 (1)	1m 22s	Rolling pastry	4y 9m 7d
5.8	4-5 (2)	13s	Counting circles of pastry	4y 9m 7d
5.9	4-5	1m 7s	Games with eggs at Easter	4y 10m 5d
5.10	4-5 (1)	31s	Counting sticks	4y 11m 18d
5.11	4-5 (2)	16s	Counting sticks	4y 11m 18d
5.12	4-5	1m 6s	Balls into sleeve	4y 11m 19d
6.1	5-6	3m 14s	Controlling remote spider	5y 6m 14d
6.2	5-6	15s	Clicking fingers	5y 1m 30d
6.3	5-6	1m 2s	Seriation explained	5y 3m 1d
6.4	5-6	30s	Playing Snakes and Ladders	5y 3m 1d

(continued)

(continued)

No.	Age Range	Duration	Description	Age in yrs, mnths and days
6.5	5-6 (1)	1m 54s	Cars and storying	5y 3m 15d
6.6	5-6 (2)	1m 30s	Cars and storying	5y 3m 15d
6.7	5-6	47s	Paper planes with cousin Harry	5y 6m 15d
6.8	5-6	1m 22s	Being 'teacher'	5y 7m 2d
6.9	5-6	1m 4s	Counting times on slide	5y 11m 28d
7.1	6-7 (1)	2m 3s	Teaching Maths	7y 14d
7.2	6-7 (2)	1m	Teaching Maths	7y 14d
7.3	6-7 (3)	53s	Teaching Maths	7y 14d
7.4	6-7	14s	Riding a motorbike	6y 1m 4d
7.5	6-7	20s	On the American Swing	6y 2m 11d
7.6	6-7	17s	Wearing 'heelies'	6y 6m 18d
7.7	6-7	25s	New guitar	6y 7m 19d
7.8	6-7	20s	Watering birdbath	6y 11m 21d
0-2	10-15 months	1m 15s	Whole and parts/pulling pegs apart and top on bottle	10-15 m

Acknowledgements

Firstly, I want to thank Gabriella, her sister, Nicole, and her parents, Evita and Paul, for their unwavering support and huge contribution throughout the writing of this book. Next, I want to thank: my 'critical friend' Colette, who always offers me helpful, constructive criticism; my husband, Terry, for some of the IT support, some scanning and photography and generally being supportive; Eloise for reminding me what it is like to have young children; and last, but not least, Beth Summers, for being at the end of the phone (and on Zoom) to give advice on behalf of the publisher.

Acknowledgements also to Magdalena Sienicka for an image (1.1) and to Martin and Marina Kraan for several images (3.2, 4.1, 4.2, 5.1 plus cover images).

Important Events/Developments in Gabby's Life

Gabby's Age Event/Development

1m 10d	First smile
3m 10d	Mum away at grandmother's funeral for three days
3m 26d	Rolls over
6m 20d	Cut her first two teeth
7m 28d	Waves
8m 11d	Plays 'Ahh-boo'
9m 7d	Claps hands
9m 20d	Shakes head to mean 'No'
14m 2d	Walks
16m 25d	Family moves house
2y 3m 19d	Starts nursery
2y 4m 15d	Mum away for three nights
2y 6m	Mop and Pop (grandparents) go to Australia for six weeks
4y 1m 6d	Family visit Latvia for two weeks
4y 2m 25d	Starts school
4y 4m 12d	Family holiday in Tenerife with Mop and Pop for one week
4y 6m 7d	Mop and Pop go to Australia for seven weeks
5y	Dad moves out of family home after he and Mum separate
5y 2m–6y 2m	Children stay with us and their Dad alternate weekends
6y	Mum away at uncle's funeral for three days
6y 2m	Dad moves into his own flat

Introduction

Family Context

Gabriella was born on 11 June 2012. I am her grandmother (Mop) and I was fortunate enough to live near her family and to be available to care for her, alongside my husband (Pop), two or three days a week when her mother went back to work.

We were away for the weekend in Bournemouth when I received a phone call at breakfast from our son, Paul, to let us know she had been born and mother and baby were well. We set off for home, only stopping to buy Gabriella a teddy on the way.

Gabriella's mother, Evita, is Latvian, so Gabby's other grandparents are a long way away. She refers to her Latvian granddad as Opi and his wife is Irina. Gabby has a big sister, Nicole, who is 4 years older and very special to Gabby.

The teddy we bought as a gift on the day of her birth became her special teddy, a 'transitional object' (Winnicott 1975) from which she could not be separated. Teddy is referred to as 'Lacitis', which is Latvian for teddy bear.

We looked after Gabriella from when she was 8 months old. Her father worked 12-hour shifts day and night, and this resulted in time off during the week when he cared for the children. Her mother returned to work part-time (9am to 3pm, Monday to Friday) and, subsequently, worked shifts during the day, which was when we cared for Gabriella.

Methodology – A Baby Biography

This book is based on the time we spent with Gabriella so is a partial picture of her development and learning, with contributions from her parents made either at the time or during the process of producing this book.

I kept a diary of anything I considered significant during Gabby's time with us. This is based on the method used by 'famous baby biographers' such as Charles Darwin and Jean Piaget. Susan Isaacs' records from an experimental school she ran during the 1920s also influence this book (Isaacs 1930).

It is important, in terms of using this method, to write down exactly what a child does and says (including gesture) as near to the event as possible and to record their age exactly (Arnold 2015). In this book, I present the ages in years (y), months (m) and days (d).

I have taken a chronological approach so following this introduction is a chapter for each year of Gabby's life until the age of seven. The themes are grounded in the data so, rather than beginning with areas of the Early Years Statutory Framework (curriculum), each chapter's headings are based on what came to the fore for Gabby that year.

Links with Theory

Whenever possible, I have analysed the observations presented by linking with a range of current theory. The basic theories that underpin my approach are as follows:

- **Attachment** – Bowlby originally conceptualized 'attachment' to carers as a survival mechanism for humans and, over the years, a great deal of research has been carried out, some of it longitudinally, that demonstrates the importance of a secure attachment to carers (Bowlby 1997). Recently, attachment theory and psychoanalysis have come together in understanding the human capacity to 'mentalize', that is 'to understand ourselves and others in terms of intentional mental states' (Fonagy et al. 2018: 1). Secure relationships formed the foundation for Gabby to develop and learn.

- **Well-being** – Laevers suggests that we consider a child's emotional well-being. Signs of well-being include 'openness and receptivity', 'vitality', 'relaxation and inner peace', and 'enjoyment without restraints' (Laevers 1997: 18–19). When a child's well-being is high, they can express a full range of emotions appropriately, so high well-being does not mean being happy all the time. Babies cry to express their needs and, as children grow, they express sadness, anger, disgust and fear as well as what might be considered the more positive emotions. A child who is emotionally healthy can express all these emotions.

- **Involvement** – this covers how involved Gabriella was in whatever she was doing, as described by Laevers et al. (2005: 10), including 'motivated', 'intense mental activity', 'satisfaction' and 'using one's exploratory drive'. We can recognize even when a young baby becomes absorbed and displays some of these signs.

- **Schemas** – according to Athey, 'a schema is a pattern of repeatable behavior into which experiences are assimilated and that are gradually co-ordinated' (2007: 50). Athey viewed schemas as 'partial concepts' (2005). Matthews (2003: 23) describes schemas like this: 'When the same or similar action is applied in different contexts and upon different objects, the child receives valuable information' about the effect of their action. It is important to notice how schemas eventually become concepts. The value of a longitudinal study, such as this, is that some links are revealed between early actions and later concepts.

- **Pedagogy** – Gabriella led her own learning insofar as a young child can, supported by adults and in an environment that afforded her explorations (Gibson 1986). I reflect on the pedagogy used in a chart at the end of each chapter. I have used the framework adopted by Ofsted by reflecting on our 'intent, implementation and impact' (Ofsted 2018).

Ethical Approach

Our relationship with Gabriella and her family is of paramount importance. Although this diary began at birth, the intention to publish has been recent and the decision was taken with the consent of Gabby and her parents. Gabriella is aware of the books I have written about my two adult grandchildren and knows that permission must be sought at each step of the way. Gabby has frequently exercised her right to ask me to delete videos she was not keen on, so I believe I am acting ethically with the best interests of Gabriella and our family at heart (Arnold 2015).

Informed consent is vital to the study, so I talked through the material with Gabby herself, and sent each section to both of her parents to read and approve. At that stage, some small changes were made at the request of the parents. My aim is to enhance our relationships, so I have followed the lead of the parents in what is appropriate and accurate to include. Release forms have been signed by Gabby and by both her parents.

With regard to anonymity, I refer to Gabby and family members by their first names. I also use the first names of Gabby's best friend at nursery (Rhea) and best friend at school (Remie). I do this for Gabby's sake, as it would not make sense to her for me to anonymize children she has such close relationships with. We have gained their parents' permission. I have used pseudonyms for other children who are referred to in the text.

I cannot predict how Gabby will feel about the book as she gets older, but the fact that she initiated it and has 'badgered' me to write it for some time means that Gabby herself owns it to some extent. As I have written books about my two older grandchildren's development and learning, as adults, they can tell me how they felt.

Georgia, whose book was published (Arnold 1999) when she was eight and is now a parent herself, says:

> I often wonder how much my love of books and reading was influenced by having a book written about me as a child. My mum tells stories of my brother and I reading out 'the funny bits' of our books to each other and laughing hysterically! Certainly, as an adult, understanding schema theory helps me to tune in to my toddler's interests and offer exciting resources that I know will appeal to him.

Harry, like, Gabby, 'badgered' me to write a book about him. He was 10 when his book was published (Arnold 2003). Harry says:

> Growing up with a family who have a great understanding of early childhood development was thoroughly advantageous. It meant they knew how to best support me, letting me explore my own interests and develop at my own pace. Having my childhood documented as part of a book has only benefited me and highlights the care and commitment given to me throughout my life. The book is a great talking point, a treasure trove of stories, and it's wonderful to have a permanent reminder of my childhood and family.

This evidences that both Georgia and Harry felt that they benefited from being the focus of a study.

Features

I present the raw observations followed by analysis in order that early childhood students might carry out their own analysis prior to reading the sense I have made of the data. There are no right or wrong versions of the analysis, as we all have our own experiences and values about how we might view a piece of data.

The book will have accompanying video clips online, which, again, provide raw data for analysis.

After presenting data and Links with Theory, I offer some provocations for practitioners under the heading 'Reflections'.

As described under 'Pedagogy' I use the framework of 'Intent, Implementation and Impact', which, again, may help practitioners to think about their responses to Ofsted.

1 Gabby's First Year

On reading through the diary I kept of Gabby's first year, certain themes emerged:

- Making relationships/communicating
- Physical development
- Cognitive development.

Naturally, there was a great deal of overlap but, for the purposes of this chapter, I offer examples of these themes.

Making Relationships/Communicating

Central to all of Gabby's learning was the forming of relationships. As a family, we were all interested in her development and encouraged Gabby to interact with us:

> At 28 days and again at 1 month 2 days, I noted that Gabby 'talked to me'.

I thought it notable when Gabby began 'smiling'. When her family were visiting our home, I noted:

> Pop (her paternal grandfather) was holding Gabby (1m 10d) and introducing her to the plants and garden. I got a hint of a *smile*.

I noted this tentatively at this point as she might just have had a bit of wind. A few days later, I was visiting her and her mother:

> Gabby (1m 15d) was asleep and woke up while I was there. I'm sure she *smiled* at me for the first time.

Again, I was a bit tentative but then became a lot more certain that she was engaging socially with me. Evita, Gabby (1m 16d) and I had been to Peterborough together. On our return to her home:

> I held Gabriella when Evita and I got back from Peterborough – she definitely *smiled* at me! Beautiful *smile*.

By now I was certain that the smile was sociable and intentional. It seemed significant that we had been together for a few hours that day. One day, there was a very different scenario. We were going to a wedding and running a bit late, so:

> I got Gabriella (2m 15d) ready. We had to wake her up and take off her babygro. She looked a bit confused and then *smiled* at me, which made it all worthwhile.

This was definitely a smile of recognition and, a few days later, I noted

> Popped to Evita and Paul's. Paul was holding Gabriella. I greeted her and she *smiled* at me (as though in recognition).

Pic 1.1 Gabby snuggled into her mum (Image by Magdalena Sienicka)

On the same day, Paul reported that 'we get lots of broad smiles first thing in the morning'.

Links with Theory

John Bowlby was the first researcher to draw our attention to 'attachment behaviour', which he defined as 'seeking and maintaining proximity to another individual' (1997: 195). He noted that young humans very quickly 'recognized their primary caregiver' and that their preference 'was extremely strong and persistent' (p.196). It was obvious that Gabby was strongly attached to her immediate family – mother, father and sister – but I was also noticing that her emotional well-being was so high that she could tolerate small changes in routine such as me waking her up and getting her dressed.

There have been several studies of babies smiling and one study of 60 Brazilian dyads linked the emergence of smiling in a baby to their mother's affective behaviour. If mothers smile at babies frequently and generally 'transmit affection', then babies tend to smile more (Mendes and Seidl-de-Moura 2014:10).

A Change in Routine

However, when Gabby was 3m 10d, her mother's grandmother died and this resulted in Evita travelling to Latvia for three days for the funeral. While Evita was away, I noted the following:

> Took dinner to Paul's and stayed till Nicole (aged 4) was settled in bed. Georgia and Harry (cousins aged 21 and 19) came around and Gabriella seemed drawn to Harry – *smiled* several times at him and studied each of them. She definitely seems to recognize me and Pop.

So Gabby seemed to cope well with her mother's short absence. However:

> I picked Evita up at the airport and couldn't wait to see Gabby's reaction on our return. She was asleep. When she stirred, Evita went over to her. She opened her eyes. Gabriella looked puzzled and then began to cry – a real, loud cry. Evita held her close and after a couple of minutes, she *smiled* at her mum.

Three days later:

> Called in this evening. I held Gabby (3m 22d) – she *smiled* at me but also kept watching and *smiling* at Nicole.

It is worth noting that, although only 4 years old, Nicole also offers security to her baby sister.

Links with Theory

Gabby's immediate family seemed to provide a 'secure base' for her and, from that base, she could explore other relationships (Bowlby 2005). Although she coped well with her mother's absence, even at her young age she was able to express her confusion and sadness on her mother's return. I believe a sign of her well-being was this expression of feelings and the fact that she soon recovered. Also, despite her young age, we talked about her mother with her while she was away. The fact that her mother understood her distress and comforted her helped her to recover.

Another Small Change

When Gabby was just over 5 months, Pop and I went on holiday for two weeks. On our return:

> Evita answered the door and Paul was holding both girls. After a minute or so, Paul passed Gabriella (5m 24d) to Pop, and Evita went to make drinks. Gabriella *smiled* at first, then her face crumpled and she cried really loudly (not a hunger cry but a real grown-up loud cry). She recovered quite quickly with Paul but the same happened when Paul handed her to me.

Following this visit, we were both ill for a few days and, therefore, did not visit. I noted:

> Went around last night. Gabriella (5m 29d) came to me first – I followed Evita into the kitchen – she was OK with me but kept her mum in sight.

So, as Bowlby pointed out, in order to maintain her security, Gabby was, with my help, maintaining proximity to her main attachment figure. A few days later, Gabby seemed excited to go into Nicole's school:

> I went around today to take Evita and Gabriella (6m) to Nicole's class for family reading. Gabby was in a great mood, *smiling*, talking, standing up, waving her dummy on its bead string. She loves being with the children, very lively, interacting and getting excited. She loves Nicole and watches/studies her.

Gabby certainly seemed to respond to the other children and especially to Nicole. She was not quite so friendly towards adults with whom she was less familiar:

> We went to Evita and Paul's for Gabriella's '6 month birthday'. She really wasn't sure of Aunty Colette and cried several times. . .

> At our house, my brother and his wife were visiting. Les took Gabby (6m 11d) onto her knee – she was OK briefly but then cried loudly.

Links with Theory

Although I have chosen 'smiling' as a theme in this first section, crying when upset or afraid is perfectly appropriate. When we consider Laevers' research on 'emotional well-being' – which can be applied to anyone of any age, based on what body language and others signs they are displaying – Gabby's responses communicate her feelings of discomfort (Laevers 1997; Laevers and Declercq 2018). She also discriminated whom she chose to smile at. She seemed to recognize that other children, although not familiar to her, were different to adults and so possibly more like her and less threatening.

Playing Peep-Bo

Evita reported:

> Gabby (7m 9d) is really enjoying peep-bo games at the moment.

This would suggest to me that she was playing with the idea of 'presence and absence' (Arnold and the Pen Green Team 2010). However, when things were not within her control:

> I looked after Gabby (7m 20d) from 9.45 till 2 in preparation for when her mother goes back to work. When we first got home, I couldn't see Pop, so knocked on the bathroom door – he popped his head out and she burst out crying.

Later on:

> Knowing she likes peep-bo, Pop tried playing ahh-boo with her but this made her cry. Is she missing Mummy and, therefore, not finding it funny to play with this idea?

Two days later, I babysat Gabriella (7m 22d) while her parents went out:

> Gabby seemed to be saying 'Mum, Mum' quite a lot. I reassured her that 'Mummy and Daddy will be back later'.

Despite her age, this seemed to reassure her.

Around the age of 7 months, Gabby seemed to develop 'waving' as a signal that people were leaving, which is important learning in terms of understanding when people are leaving:

> I looked after Gabriella (7m 28d) for a short time at their house as Paul was going to bed in preparation for nightshift. Paul said 'bye-bye' and waved. Gabby waved her arms up and down. Then when he was going to bed, he waved and said 'bye' again and she waved.

In this instance, I noted that 'meaning is being constructed in the space between them' as Vygotsky explained with 'pointing' (1978: 55).

By now, I was caring for Gabby two or three days a week:

> When Gabby was in her seat having lunch in our living room, she studied everything on our mantelpiece, including family photos. I talked about Mummy (at work), Daddy (in bed) and Nicole (at school). I promised to make a book that week.

This is where my 'intent' came in, as I intentionally talked about Gabby's close family, reminding her that we had taken Nicole to school and Mummy to work and would pick them up later to go to their home (Ofsted 2018). I also intended to make a photobook for Gabby so that she could easily join in that conversation by pointing and possibly vocalizing how she was feeling away from her immediate family. I was 'implementing' by talking about the family initially. My hope was that she would begin to understand the new routine was us looking after her when her parents were at work.

It was not surprising when I noted:

> Looked after Gabby (8m 11d) most of the day and spent it at home with Pop. I'm convinced she's playing ahh-boo because she lifts both arms and whatever she's holding (dummy, pegs, cloth, Daddy's shift pattern) and then lowers them and laughs.

I saw this as a good sign that, once again, she was playing a kind of 'here and gone' game. Gabby may have been symbolizing, in a very simple way, the idea of 'presence and absence' at a time when her main carers were absent, showing that she was beginning to process this (Shaw 2019).

However, during the same day,

> My brother visited and Gabby was really wary of him and cried when he spoke quite loudly . . . also cried when Pop pretended to cry . . . and lots of saying 'Mama' today.

I think this shows that her security with us was still quite fragile. A few days later, her mother reported that 'Gabriella's feeling jealous when me and Nicole cuddle and cries and wants to join in'.

The Book

A few days later:

> I looked after Gabby (8m 16d) for a couple of hours at their home. She got excited when I went in. I'd made a book with photos of Gabriella, her Mum, Dad and Nicole. I gave it to her – she seemed to like it, opening and closing it, looking at the photos and then put the corner of the book into her mouth. Then she noticed her name on the cover was not fully stuck down. She seems to be paying attention to detail and edges, labels etc. She managed to pull her name off. Then she ripped it in half and then ripped one half in half again. Then spent about five minutes trying to rip these three small pieces in half. Finally started putting the small pieces of paper in her mouth. At this point, we took the pieces of paper from her.

Gabby's first response to the book was what I expected, examining it, deducing what kind of object it was – a book similar to other books, noticing but not necessarily focusing on the photos. Then she became totally involved in separating her name from the book (because she could) (Laevers 1997). Her involvement in tearing the paper was intense and prolonged for a child of her age. Five minutes is a long time to concentrate on something. It would have been easy for me to pursue my agenda, drawing Gabby's attention to the photos and continuing with the conversation I hoped would develop. However, at this point, I paused and 'took a step back' so to speak, and thought carefully about what Gabby was trying to do. I also tried to think about how I could enable her to do what she was trying to do. So, at this point, her **intent** influenced my actions.

After this, I reprinted the names and laminated them. I attached Velcro to the book and to each name so that Gabby could separate them from the book with some effort. Also, she could put them into her mouth without choking but she could not tear the names. However, the theme of 'separating' and connecting continued with other objects and paper (see Physical Development and Cognitive Development).

Reflections

Have you ever noticed children either rejecting something you have offered or doing something unexpected with what you offer them?

How have you responded?
Whose agenda is generally at the forefront of your mind?
Would it help to pause and think about what children are trying to do?

Continuing to Make and Understand Relationships

Gabriella (8m 25d):

Had a mirror with handles – used it to play peep-bo with Paul – did it intentionally.

Also:

Seems to wave consistently when we wave and say 'bye', even when Paul is going upstairs to bed (as her father works shifts he often goes to bed during the day).

Gabriella played with her book quite a lot and sometimes focused on the photos:

Gabby (9m 11d) looked at her book, did more looking at pics and pointing.

An Emergency Situation

When Gabriella was 9m 14d:

Family have had a traumatic weekend – Paul was working days and forgot his phone. Nicole had tummy pains and was admitted to hospital. Evita forgot her purse and ended up being alone at the hospital for hours with both children. Could not contact us as we were at the theatre. Eventually, Evita rang Colette who went over and brought Gabby home. She had no car seat so had to get a lift and hold Gabby, who fell asleep in her arms. Georgia and Harry came around and Georgia reported that Gabby would not eat or play but just wanted to be held. She seemed OK till Paul walked in, when she burst into tears (of relief?).

Despite being wary of Colette previously, even at 9 months Gabriella seemed to sense that this was an emergency situation. Evita ended up staying overnight at the hospital. Colette popped around the following evening and says that Gabriella was grinning at her as though she knew her. I would like to think that it is these small challenges that begin to build resilience in young children. According to Hornor (2017: 385), 'exposure to mild or moderate stress . . . may actually be beneficial to development (Rutter 2013)'.

Other Children

I took Gabriella to a baby drop-in session:

Gabriella (10m 5d) was OK but quiet until three parents with 2-year-olds came in, when she became very animated. Trying to communicate with and fascinated by them.

I noted a few weeks later:

Went to the children's centre with Gabriella (11m 25d) this morning – it was baby massage. Gabby liked the other babies and the massage doll, which was quite big and cumbersome.

Links with Theory

Colwyn Trevarthen (2002) has shown that babies are born wanting to communicate and to share the culture of their families. This is facilitated by parents, who intuitively adopt 'parentese' or 'infant-directed speech' (IDS), a kind of high-pitched speech rhythm that communicates perfectly with babies. Although I did not note that adults used this kind of tone when communicating with Gabby, I am sure that they did. Even more interesting is her obvious recognition of, and excitement when, interacting with other children.

Physical Development

With regard to the current version of *Development Matters* (DfE 2020), we observed Gabby's physical development unfold very much in line with what this document outlines:

> From the age of 23 days, Gabby showed a preference for being held upright and facing outwards.

There were several mentions of this preference in my diaries. So, as well as her wish to watch whatever was going on, she was supported in an upright position, the same position she had retained in the womb, as she was in a breech position and born by an emergency caesarean operation. I noticed:

> Gabriella (2m 26d) using her hands more, in mouth, gripping my T-shirt and fingers. She was playing with Paul's fingers when he lay her down on the couch. Paul says she often plays with Evita's fingers but not usually with his.

A few days later, we popped in when both girls were being bathed:

> Gabriella (3m) was really enjoying being in the water, kicking legs, waving arms and squealing and smiling.

A further development was manipulating objects:

> Gabby (3m 16d) is playing with her dummy, focusing on it and bringing it towards her mouth, occasionally managing to get it in, then takes it out and puts it back in.

Then:

> Gabby (3m 22d) held her dummy in one hand and spent ages trying to get her other hand to it. She also pushed to stand up on my knee and felt quite strong and steady.

Links with Theory

According to Athey, 'our actions become our thinking', so every action that Gabby found she could do and practise was significant to her overall development (1990, 2007). We can see here that, at first, she grasped fingers. Those fingers co-operate with her intention, reminding me very much of Vygotsky's idea that we learn in co-operation with more capable others. In this example, when Gabby is grasping an adult's fingers, the adult makes them available and is likely to reconnect when she lets go. Grasping her dummy is more of a challenge and she is also trying to co-ordinate grasping with movement to her mouth and with bringing both hands to an object simultaneously. Her involvement is high, suggesting that she is engaging in 'deep-level learning' (Laevers 1997).

A Further Development

I wrote:

> Big news today – Gabriella (3m 26d) rolled over onto her tummy this morning at home.

Within a few days, with lots of practice, she was becoming really adept:

> Two days ago, Gabriella (4m 3d) rolled onto her tummy and then rolled back over onto her back.

I also noted that:

> Gabriella likes to hold things – she now has her dummy on a string of beads to attach to her clothes – she was holding her beads and waving her arms and clonked herself (I also noted that 'she doesn't realize the consequences of that action yet').

> Nicole was eating crisps and gave Gabriella the empty packet to hold. Gabby loved holding the packet, squeezing and scrunching it, putting it in her mouth, smelling it. It kept her engaged for a good few minutes.

A few days later, (when she was 4m 7d), I wrote:

> Puzzling over Gabriella's actions – she waves her arms up and down because she can. Already, she is co-ordinating two actions, grasping and the up/down movement. She does it with everything she can get her hands on.

Links with Theory

Gabriella was making major leaps in development at this time so it was not surprising that a couple of days later, at 4m 9d, she had a bad day:

> Evita and Paul said it had been a bad day – crying even when they went out for a walk – she just wanted to be held.

Brazelton and Sparrow (2006) explain that 'touchpoints are critical moments in a child's development' and that often, when learning something new, there are changes in behaviour and regression may occur in other areas. In terms of schema theory, we can clearly see Gabby repeating actions, such as 'grasping' and moving objects in an 'up/down trajectory' and co-ordinating these actions (Athey 2007). Rolling over is also a major achievement.

Grabbing

These co-ordinations continued, including holding objects and putting them in her mouth, for example the remote control, teething ring, wooden puzzle and food. However, the grasping or holding became 'grabbing' and became more refined:

Gabby (4m 20d) grabbed my glasses, nose and ear.

Four days later:

She grabbed my earring (the ring type).

I observed that Gabby (4m 26d):

Grabbed her own feet and also grabbed a cup from her mum and made as though to drink from it.

Gabby would regularly try to grab my glasses and necklace. Nicole told me 'she's a grabber' at 6 months. On one occasion, I noted:

Gabby (6m 11d) grabbed my glasses and necklace. I took my necklace off and she played with it, holding it and moving her arm up and down and watching the beads move before putting them in her mouth.

Links with Theory

Here, Gabby was studying the effect of her actions. This is what Athey referred to as 'functional dependency relationships' (1990: 70). The beads moving were dependent on Gabby moving her arms up and down. At this stage, she seemed to be observing the effect of her repeated action, rather than knowing what would happen.

Providing More Resources for Gabby to Explore

At our home, I introduced a metal mixing bowl and some pegs. At Gabby's home, she had access to a treasure basket, as recommended by Elinor Goldschmied (1987), containing natural objects to be explored by babies who are sitting up. Gabby (6m 20d) cut her first two teeth. She continued exploring with her hands and mouth and I noted:

> Gabby (7m 5d) is sitting up almost independently; moves her tongue in and out of her mouth; played with pegs and bowl. I added a lemon but it was a bit too big for her to pick up. Her favourite thing was picking the bowl up containing the pegs and banging it on the floor.

At 7m 9d:

> Pop sat her between his feet and gave her his iPhone. She touches it and seems to notice the changes. She scrapes her fingers across the screen and puts it in her mouth.

I also noted that 'Gabby is eating normal food mashed'. I encouraged her to feed herself as I had done with my own children as, although it would be a bit messy to begin with, I was sure she would soon develop the skills with practice.

At 8m 16d, she:

> held two coasters from the treasure basket, one in each hand. She banged one against the other. She also banged one with a dolly peg. Gabby got several objects out of the treasure basket but kept going back to the two coasters. Then she picked out a large wooden spoon and waved it from side to side by turning her wrist. Did the same with a large whisk. She moved the whole treasure basket forward and back (away from and towards herself) – it was quite heavy and full.

Within the next couple of days, she:

> tried to pick up small pieces of paper, which were on the floor; held a large flag, put her finger in a hole in the corner of the flag and tried to pull it apart (pulling from side to side); sat with Pop and ripped an old *Radio Times*, again using a side-to-side movement (very involved and focused when doing this).

Links with Theory

I think we oversimplify in thinking that children move from exploring gross motor movements to fine motor movements but I think these observations demonstrate that Gabby was trying out these movements simultaneously. The Early Years Foundation Stage (EYFS) does state that 'children show good control and co-ordination in large and small movements' (DfE 2017). I underlined her use of 'turning her wrist' to make a long object move from side to side as this was something new, which she subsequently applied to a large whisk. This movement may have been adopted because of the weight of the spoon and then used on a similar object. Athey pointed out that the horizontal drawing movement follows the vertical drawing movement in terms of development so it is logical to presume that the side-to-side movement develops after the up/down movement (Athey 1990: 79) and this seemed to be the case in observations of Gabby.

Becoming More Mobile and Stronger

Between 9 and 12 months, Gabby became much faster at moving herself around on her bottom. Her explorations also became more refined and she frequently practised more refined movements. For example, at 9m 30d, I noted:

> Really into books, opening, closing, pointing.

And then:

> Gabby (10m 6d) moved herself towards our hearth – took a small drawer out and removed four small bottles of essential oil.
>
> (At home) Gabby (10m 13d) is whizzing around the room using both hands to propel herself.

At our house:

> Gabby (10m 20d) shuffled on her bum all the way to the kitchen and to the doorway of the conservatory – she was very excited, waving arms and legs up and down. . .'

On the same day, 'she systematically pulled apart 13 small pegs' (using her side-to-side movement).
I filmed Gabby (10m 27d):

> Amazing!! She spent seven minutes trying to put a top on a bottle.

Her mother reported:

> Nicole was upstairs – Gabby (11m 8d) shuffled to the bottom of the stairs and pulled herself up to standing at the bottom of the stairs.

At 11m 25d:

> Seemed to be trying things out with two pegs (or more) in hands –
> beating 'drum', carrying and throwing, becoming more deliberate.
> Approached wooden box and took out two drawers – realized
> there was a round handle on each drawer – hung drawer on finger
> by putting finger through handle.

Reflections

Think about how you encourage the physical development of children in your setting or in children that you know.

What sorts of resources help physical development?
Think about your role in helping babies to feed themselves.

Cognitive Development

The word 'cognitive' implies that babies come to know things. Dictionary definitions of 'cognition' include:

> act or experience of knowing or acquiring knowledge (Collins 2006)
>
> something known or perceived (thefreedictionary.com)

Some definitions mention 'memory', 'learning', 'judgement' and 'reasoning'. It is my belief that, as human beings, we are constantly adapting to the environments in which we find ourselves and that we do that by assimilating experiences and accommodating to new experiences (von Glasersfeld 1995).

I would also make the point that 're-cognition' involves 'cognition' because it requires memory. So, in the section on 'Making relationships' in this chapter, Gabby was demonstrating from quite early on that she 're-cognised' certain people who were familiar to her. This provided some evidence that she was using her memory.

So my criteria for including examples in this section on Gabby's cognitive development are:

- recognition of people
- the emergence of language, including putting two ideas together (e.g. when she heard us say something and looked towards the object/person or gestured)
- intentionality, especially when we observed her repeat her actions.

Recognizing People

I noticed that Gabby (23d):

> looked right at me today as though she was studying my face.

At 1 month 16 days, she:

> definitely smiled at me.

This was a smile of recognition noted on many occasions with immediate family (see section on 'Making relationships') and this was very different to her reaction to people with whom she was less familiar. We also noticed that Gabby seemed, from a young age, to discern that she could accept and be friendly towards other children even though she might be coming into contact with them for the first time. So, it was that they were strangers to her but that they belonged to the category of 'children' or 'young people', and that she could tell the difference. Gabby probably did this by looking (children have smaller frames than adults), listening (their softer voices with a high pitch are possibly similar to 'parentese') and also by assessing the reactions of adults to other children and of children to her. I cannot find any studies in the literature on this topic, although Judy Dunn has closely studied sibling relationships.

Links with Theory

As far as developing memory is concerned Alison Gopnik (2009) states that 'infants have specific memories of particular events' (p.138). So, in effect, they link events together and gradually their story becomes more joined up, detailed and coherent. What babies do seem to remember is what happened with particular people or in certain situations. Gopnik also points out that, for young children, the language used by adults around them helps with that process in the sense of drawing attention to certain events.

Developing Language

The first mention in the diary of Gabby developing noticeably different expressive sounds was when Paul reported that:

> Gabby (2m 26d) has been making a 'roaring' sound (using her voice).

At 3 months, I noted that she recognized her own name:

> Very aware of me and Pop and seemed to respond to her name.

Also around this time:

> Just before the family left our house, Gabriella (3m 3d) was lying on the couch and 'talking' to Paul. I captured a few seconds on video.

Although it is generally recognized that television and digital devices do not play a major role in teaching children language, I noted that:

> Gabby (5m) is engaging with large-headed figures on TV and wants to watch those rather than me.

At our house:

> On Pop's knee, Gabby (5m 29d) got excited about what was on TV, making sounds, 'talking' and laughing.

The whole family came around for dinner and, on this occasion, Gabby (6m 26d) was able to sit at the table:

> Gabby spent most of the time talking and joining in. She was really making lots of different sounds. We were speculating about which sounds/words she would say first. There were definitely 'baba' and 'mm' sounds. She was very animated and stayed there joining in until we all moved (about an hour).

I was babysitting when Gabby (7m 22d) showed an interest in TV:

> What surprised me was her interest in kids' TV. She especially seemed to like *Peppa Pig* and, each time the theme tune came on, she waved her arms up and down and got excited.

Her receptive language was developing well as I observed:

> At our house Pop mentioned Teddy Tim and Gabriella (7m 24d) looked straight at the teddy (regularly referred to as 'Teddy Tim').

And a day later:

> Saying 'dadada' to Teddy Tim.

At 7m 28d, the specific sounds Gabby was expressing seemed to be associated with certain people. I noticed:

> Different sounds today – lots of gargling sounds and 'rrr' and only 'mama' when Evita was home and a bit of 'baba' when Nicole was there.

Gabby recognized other theme tunes as well as *Peppa Pig*. At 8m 25d, she:

> seemed to recognize the theme tunes of *Friends* and of *Two and a Half Men*.

> When Pop mentioned Teddy Tom (a smaller teddy she was holding), Gabby (9m 2d) looked at Teddy Tom.

and also that day, she started:

> making a 'kkkee' sound I've not heard before.

At 9m 11d:

> Lots of talking especially 'ga . . . ga . . . ga' – I sang 'ga . . . ga . . . gaga' and she almost sang it back to me.

It was Easter Sunday and we were out at a park. Gabby (9m 20d) fought sleep but eventually dropped off to sleep. Back at their house I noticed that:

> Gabby seemed to shake her head appropriately to mean 'no'.

Gesture played an important part in our communications:

> Gabby (10m 19d) knows what the word 'kiss' means. Twice in conversation, I used the word 'kiss' and each time she turned to me with her mouth open to 'kiss' me (in her fashion).

Links with Theory

Recent research studies agree that there is an innate component when it comes to learning language and that the environment provides the language to learn. We are born with the building blocks to learn any language to which we are exposed. As Gopnik et al. state: 'Rather, nature and nurture are inseparably entwined' when it comes to learning language (1999: 131). According to Malloch and Trevarthen, 'communicative musicality' is a strong factor in how easily young children learn language (2009).

As well as music, rhyme and story, the way adults intuitively interact with babies using 'parentese' helps children to learn language. Each interaction is a kind of narrative and developing the back and forth of a conversation with babies is an important part of the process of learning to communicate. In a recent paper produced by Early Education, Asmussen points out that 'children's understanding of language begins at 23 weeks' gestation when the foetus can first hear the mother's voice and other sounds outside the womb (Moore and Linthicum 2007)' (2019: 5). Asmussen also indicates certain milestones, for example 'babbling at 6 months' and babies recognizing that their name refers to them is also at around 6 months. She also refers to a 'watershed moment' when infants learn to point, at around 10 months.

Recognition, Noticing and Intentionality

As we have seen, Gabby remembered familiar people and showed signals such as smiling to indicate she knew and trusted certain people. Apart from recognizing people, the first observation in the diary that definitely indicated Gabby was taking note of somewhere different was when we were at a wedding at a country house (Wadenhoe House):

> Gabby (2m 12d) seemed to notice the lovely building and looked up at it several times.

It helped that she was being carried 'facing out and upright', for which she had shown a preference.

I have documented many of her repeated actions in the section on physical development, such as 'grasping' and 'holding' objects, 'grabbing', up/down trajectory movements, side-to-side movements and the beginning of a kind of rotating movement when holding a wooden spoon and whisk.

Links to Theory

In 1990, Athey wrote that, 'The associated notion (at the heart of Piaget's theories), that "thought" is "internalized action" has been slow to be adopted as a research hypothesis probably because it is difficult to test' (p.33). Athey's observations trace the journey from action to thought across a group of 20 children aged 2 to 5 years.

In this study of Gabby, we can see the actions emerging, being repeated and beginning to co-ordinate during her first year.

Understanding the Effect of Her Actions

At times, Gabby seems to be predicting what might happen as a result of her actions or the actions of others:

> Paul reported that at home Gabby (7m 9d) presses the remote control and looks towards the TV. Even if she's facing away from it, she'll turn and look at the TV immediately after pressing the remote control.

This seems to indicate that Gabby had some understanding of what happens as a result of pressing the buttons on the remote, what Athey refers to as 'functional dependency relationships' (1990: 69).

> We were in Asda supermarket when Gabby (7m 28d) noticed that the blind/shutter was coming down on the hairdresser's shop. She then looked above each shop in turn (expecting the other blinds to come down?).

I noticed:

> Gabby (8m 16d) put to her mouth anything 'cup' shaped.

This observation shows that Gabby was able to recognize containers and understood one of their functions (to drink from).

Inevitably, some of Gabby's actions relate to what she has observed her sister doing. For example, Paul reported:

> Gabriella (8m 24d) was sitting on the floor trying to put on Nicole's 'Minnie ears' for a long time and was very happy when she saw herself in the mirror with them on.

Gabby (9m 3d) played with Teddy Tim's knitted scarf. I filmed her waving the scarf:

> She was pulling it, putting it on her head and occasionally around her back or neck. She was very involved.

Soon after:

> Gabriella can clap and practises. Was doing it to show me.

Clapping may seem like a simple achievement that all humans and some primates can automatically do but it involves a co-ordination of the side-to-side movements we saw Gabby practising in other ways and also involves moving each hand in an opposite direction and towards the other hand and connecting repeatedly. Apart from the physical actions, Gabby also knows when it is appropriate to clap.

Having observed Gabby with the scarf first-hand and repeatedly (as I filmed the sequence), I offered her the magnetic necklace I was wearing but she got it in a tangle. I also offered her a chain from the treasure basket.

> Gabby briefly held it and shook it in an up/down movement. I questioned: 'Is it too different from Teddy's scarf?'

Evita noticed Gabby co-ordinating two actions when:

> Evita had given Gabby (9m 14d) the little box of (Community Playthings) baby blocks. Her mum tipped them on the floor. Gabby put one block into the empty box and shook it (as though to hear the sound?), which Evita thought was clever. Evita got the box down while I was there and Gabriella did the same several times with different blocks – a co-ordination of containing and trajectory.

This thread of thinking continued when Gabby was at our house at 9m 28d:

> Played with pegs and shuffled over to empty Easter egg box and put peg in, then got frustrated trying to get it back out.

Two days later:

> I provided a small gift box. I put a peg inside and closed the lid. Gabby tried to open it and then rejected it. A bit later I left it open with the peg inside. She immediately picked it up and shook it up and down exactly as she had done with the block and box at home. Shook the peg out and repeated three or four times, putting the peg in, shaking up and down. Rejected a dolly peg as it did not fit as easily.

These sorts of actions became part of her repertoire, frequently repeated with different content, for example when Gabby (10m 18d) played 'putting small cup inside larger cup and shaking it till the smaller cup fell out'; 11m 4d with 'a ball in a cup' and at 11m 8d when she 'put all of Duplo into container. They were all over the room. Threw each block in and was excited'.

Another interest around this time was recognizing where things go, labelled by some researchers as 'positionality' (Grimmer, 2017) or 'orientation' (England, 2018):

> Gabby (9m 21d) tried to put her hat on her own head.

> At 10 months at our house, Nicole had taken her shoes off. Gabby leaned over and got one shoe, lifted her foot and put shoe near it – did this three times. Also undid Velcro on my shoe and put Nicole's shoe near my foot. At Evita's, was playing with her mum's hoop earrings and twice put an earring near her own ear.

A New Pattern to Explore Emerges

The first time I noted Gabby's interest in 'circularity' and 'rotating', she was 10m 13d, when she:

> went over to Nicole's buggy, moved it, looking at wheels.

Four days later:

> Gabriella picked up a recorder, turned it around, put right end in mouth, blew it and made sounds. Looked pleased – did it several times. When she put the recorder on the floor, it rolled away from her. She seemed interested in it rolling. Earlier, she moved Nicole's pram, looking at the wheels. Got out wooden car – examined the wheels.

Gabriella added this interest to her repertoire and continued to notice objects that could rotate including 'throwing and rolling balls' and 'a rotating chair' at 11m 9d; 'attracted to a rotating mirror toy' at 11m 11d.

Links with Theory

I have focused on actions and objects that provoked Gabby's interest, as shown in her involvement and pleasure in whatever she was doing (Laevers 1997). I find it impossible to ignore the repeated patterns of action which she became engaged in exploring (Athey 1990, 2007; Atherton and Nutbrown 2013). It seemed obvious in this section that Gabby was gradually adding to her repertoire of schemas. The big question is whether interests were provoked by the environment including people or were innate. Athey (2013: 6) states that 'all learning has its inner and outer aspects'. She goes on to explain that 'children learn through experience' but that:

> real experiencing always requires the cognitive or thinking participation of the learner either consciously or non-consciously.

So I would deduce that, like language, other learning involves nature and nurture and our job, as early year professionals and parents, is to notice what is emerging and 'feed' it with suitable content and language. Atherton and Nutbrown (2016) refer to 'schematic pedagogy' as 'taking time to attune to children's own significances' (p.76). This is precisely what we were attempting to do with Gabby.

Reflections

Think about the last time you were with a child or group of children and ask yourself:

How carefully did I observe what the child/children were interested in?
What language did I use when interacting?
How did the child/children respond?
Which resources did I introduce?

SUMMARY

This first chapter traces Gabby's development and learning during her time with us, as grandparents, and includes many conversations with her parents. It presents data on:

- making relationships
- physical development
- cognitive development.

We also see the emergence of schemas Gabby is exploring:

- Grasping and holding
- Up/down trajectory movements

- Side-to-side or horizontal trajectory movements
- Containing
- Rotating
- Co-ordinations of (for example) containing and trajectory.

As far as pedagogy is concerned:

Intent	Implementation	Impact
Supporting Gabby's language development and relationship forming	Talking to Gabby using 'parentese'	She engages with and 'talks' to us
Following her lead or intent	For example, holding her upright and facing out	Gabby notices aspects of the environment, e.g. a different building
Talking about where her parents and sister are when they are not with her	Making a family photo book and looking at it with her, providing language to describe where they are and that they will come back	Gabby begins to understand separations from close attachment figures
Noticing her interest in up/down movement	Offering new content, e.g. necklace, chain and language to match her actions	Gabby learns about 'up/down' and about 'tangles' and rejects content too different to what she was interested in exploring (e.g. a scarf)
Seeing the possibility for co-ordinating schemas	Offering containers and objects to be contained and language to match	Containing and trajectory become part of Gabby's repertoire

2   From 1 to 2 Years

On reading through all the data of this period, when Gabby and I spent a great deal of time together, two dominant themes emerged:

- The learning of receptive and expressive language.
- Repeated patterns of action – the seeking of variables, functional dependency relationships, symbolic play and accommodations.

Receptive and Expressive Language

As I pointed out in Chapter 1, children are learning language from when they are in the womb (Asmussen 2019). However, this period between 1 and 2 years, when children become more mobile, is when they can really demonstrate their understanding of what is being said. What struck me first was how frequently Gabby used gesture, either to demonstrate her understanding or, more often, to communicate her preferences and to get her needs met.

Gesture

Here are some examples of gesture. At 13m 11d:

Can nod as well as shake her head.

At 14 m 23d:

Asked for music by pointing.

Many times, I noted down how Gabby expressed her emotions by gesture and movement, for example:

After getting a small empty bottle out of the wooden box and blowing it, I got out bubbles and blew them. Gabby (15m 20d) was really excited, jumping up and down and squealing with excitement while trying to catch the bubbles.

As well as letting me know what she wanted, she was very good at telling me what she did not want. We were at a parent and child group when she got her top wet:

> At home time, I tried to put a borrowed top on Gabby (17m 25d) and she cried very loudly.

The family moved house when Gabby was 16m 25d. It was 3 months after this that Gabby showed signs of not wanting people to leave and not wanting to say goodbye. On one occasion, we had gone to their home for dinner. I noted:

> Gabby (19m 21d) is practising facial expressions and bodily gestures. When we said 'we're going home now', she put her head down, two hands on her face and shook her head (did the same the day before when Pop announced he was going shopping).

Two days later:

> Would not say goodbye to Nicole at school and shook her head.

I was not sure why she became reluctant to say goodbye or to let people go home after being with her at this point, as it was a while after they moved house and they were mostly seeing the same people. One week, I did not see much of her as her parents were off work for a few days:

> Popped in to see the family tonight and Gabby (21m 16d) came straight to me and stayed on my knee with her head on my chest for a good ten minutes (she must have missed me!).

Sometimes, Gabby would mirror, in gesture, what she had observed. We were visiting East Carlton Park, where there are ducks and a lake:

> Gabby (20m 8d) got excited when watching the ducks. Wiggled her bum when the ducks shook water off their bodies.

At this stage, she would sometimes 'frown and make noises' when children came near her in the soft-play room (21 m 1d). Gabby was also very good at showing her delight when she did something she was pleased with:

> Took Gabriella (21m 7d) to West Glebe Park. She loved going up the steps and down the slide. She showed signs of being 'chuffed' – giggling and doing a little dance. She did not want to leave.

When we were sharing stories, she would show clear preferences for certain books and parts of stories. Gabby (23m 2d) had chicken-pox so we were staying at home,

> When Gabby woke up, she played with books. She now likes *Where Do Baby Animals Come From?* (having previously rejected it). Also looked at a book Nicole had made and (another favourite book), *The Baby's Catalogue*. She has favourite bits that she always comments on, for example, she gestures the baby playing 'peep-bo' when looking at *The Baby's Catalogue*.

Links with Theory

Kettner and Carpendale (2013), in a study of eight children, report that nodding the head comes later than shaking the head, usually at around 16–18 months. However, they point out that the physical movement comes before the understanding of what the gesture means. So, at this point, Gabby may have just been practising the gesture rather than using it to communicate.

Tait (2005) carried out a study of 'chuffedness as an indicator of quality in an early childhood setting' and found that young children know and celebrate when they learn something new or master something that has challenged them. Chuffedness could be seen as the sheer joy and satisfaction children feel when they challenge themselves and achieve what they have set out to do.

I look once more to attachment theory to explain why Gabby became resistant to people leaving (Bowlby 1997). Hellos and good-byes are important rituals for young children to learn. In the Growing Together group for parents with their children at the Pen Green Centre, the staff always greet parents and children individually and, towards the end of each session, those who can manage it blow bubbles to signal that the session is coming to an end and that it is time to go home or elsewhere (Cole and Gallagher 2018). Through doing this every week, even very young children get used to the bubbles as a signal that the group is ending. We saw in Chapter 1 how confused and upset Gabby was by her mum's three days away. By this age (21 months), she was possibly able to understand a little more about my absence for a few days, though keen to show she had missed me.

Music

Another theme that became apparent when going through the data was how often music and singing, often accompanied by actions, contributed to Gabby learning language. Gabby heard music at home, probably some of it more modern than the music I played. I made a point of playing a variety of music at my house, ranging from classical to musicals. In addition, we attended a weekly parent/carer singing group and towards the end of this year another group which ended with nursery action rhymes.

> Gabby (12m 20d) was a bit out of sorts today but excited to hear Maori music.

This was a CD I played regularly and that she recognized. Occasionally, when I introduced something new, she could be unsure at first:

> I played 'Mamma Mia' for the first time. Gabby (12m 22d) cried briefly but then danced, clapped, banging legs on floor and moving head.

One day, when Nicole was unwell, I looked after both children at their home:

> Gabby (13m 6d) looked at her books and listened to 17 tunes on Nicole's CD player. She stood at the table and clapped.

Gabby would frequently ask for music by pointing or jigging. Gabby walked for the first time at 14m 2d. At her home:

> Gabby (14m 23d) asked for music by pointing and trying to climb on the couch – she knows which two buttons to press for the music to play. It was September but she played 'Jingle Bells' and marched around waving both arms up and down (her version of dancing).

When I put on music by The Beach Boys:

> Gabby (15m 1d) danced with Teddy Tim, mostly going around and around.

Her dad reported that Gabby (15m 8d) recognized the word 'music'. There was a strong emotional connection to music for Gabby so, when her parents were preparing to move house:

> Evita told me Gabby (16m 24d) was most upset when she packed the music centre. Gabby kept pointing at the box.

However, the following day:

> I took the girls home to their new house – we went in the back door – one of the first things Gabby noticed was the music centre on the side in the kitchen. I wrote 'Let's hope that's a good connector for her.'

As time went on, Gabby became familiar with, and joined in with, action rhymes at both groups we attended. She also made connections between singing and enacting those rhymes and the rhymes in books.

> We'd been to a group where Gabby (20m 27d) most enjoyed the songs and rhymes at the end. She joined in with the actions and, as we went to the car, seemed to be re-enacting what she'd done at the group. In the car, she looked at a rhyme book and kept pointing at a spider so I sang 'Incy Wincy Spider'.

Links with Theory

According to Malloch and Trevarthen (2009), music is the oldest form of communication. They say that music is older than language and, as such, it seems no surprise that young children learn through music. They found that 'parentese' or 'infant-directed speech' is musical. Parents, carers and even children intuitively adopt this way of speaking to babies across cultures.

Cirelli et al. (2018) report that 'musical interactions are a source of important social information to infants' (p.66). They point out that infants learn about their culture through music and that young children are especially skilled at 'detecting meter changes' (that is, subtle changes in the number of beats or slight changes in the pattern) that adults might not perceive (p.67). Although I am writing this account from my perspective as a grandparent, I know that Evita sang lullabies in Latvian, thereby valuing Gabby's bicultural background.

Understanding

There were several mentions of Gabby understanding what we were saying. For example, Paul reported:

> Whenever I say 'I'm going to change your nappy', Gabby (14m 26d) immediately goes to the cupboard where the nappies are kept.

> Also, if I said 'Take your socks off', she follows that instruction.

We also noticed that if one of the toys was mentioned, Gabby responded:

> At her house, when I mentioned Baby Annabelle, Gabby (14m 30d) went straight over and lifted up the doll.

The fact that she was now walking probably made her understanding more obvious to us. We also began to notice that she could remember some information or instruction:

> We were in the kitchen and I said something about 'getting Teddy's trousers'. Gabby (16m 3d) went all the way into the living room (far end), picked up the trousers and brought them to me.

The following day, we were attending a group session at a children's centre, when I told her:

> You 'could put the frog in the water', which she did, although the water was at the other side of the room. Then 'You could get a towel to dry the frog', which, again, she understood and held in mind while going around other children to the other side of the room.

On another occasion, I noted that her understanding enabled her to defer gratification:

> We walked to the little post office. Gabby (19m 2d) stopped at the park on the way. She wanted to go in and play. I explained we could do that on the way back after we had been to the post office. She seemed to understand.

Again, Gabby (22m 14d) demonstrated her understanding of an explanation:

> At Growing Together, Gabby had watched Cessie sharpening pencils. Gabby had a go but tended to twist the sharpener both ways. Cessie guided her hand to keep rotating in one direction. They sharpened all the pencils, but Gabby did not want to stop or to give the sharpener back to Cessie. I explained that 'Cessie needs to put the sharpener away in the cupboard, then I need to change your nappy and then it's bubbles'. She thought for a second, then handed the sharpener to Cessie.

Links with Theory

Children seem to have this amazing ability to learn language without really trying, as long as they are exposed to it. Recent studies confirm that social interaction is important (Lake and Evangelou 2019). Experimental studies using brain-imaging techniques demonstrated that 'the degree of infants' social engagement during sessions predicted both phonetic and word learning' (Kuhl 2010: 721). Other aspects are the 'relationship' between people as they interact and also the fact that very young children are assisted by the 'gaze' of their partner or partners (Kuhl 2010). So, although television and digital media can assist a bit with learning language, those means are nowhere near as powerful as human interactions (Kuhl 2010). The likelihood is that Gabby was picking up language from birth and before but that she could not necessarily demonstrate her understanding to us until she was mobile. It is believed that there is a 'critical period' for learning language and that, during the first few months, babies are receptive to all language sounds.

Expression

A first word that Gabriella said with meaning was 'more' (at 12m 7d). Another word that she could not quite say but attempted was 'round and round'. Her version at 13m 8d was 'ra ra'. On this occasion:

> Sitting outside for lunch, Gabriella was very interested in a spinning ladybird, flowers and butterflies. I talked to her about the ladybird going 'round and round'. She seemed to repeat, saying 'ra ra'. Then I did 'round and round the garden' and she giggled, anticipating being tickled.

Here I was trying to help Gabby make conceptual links between things that go around and the action of rotating. She subsequently adopted the term 'ra ra' when initiating 'round and round the garden' and also when she saw a water wheel (at 14m 17d). According to Matthews (2003: 29), the language we offer acts as a 'pivot' in the brain to hold together repeated actions and to form concepts.

The other strong motivator for expressing language, unsurprisingly, was people. Paul reported:

> We have a gate at the bottom of the stairs now and when her mum was upstairs the other day, Gabby (13m 29d) was at the bottom saying 'Mummmummmum' repeatedly. When he was telling me, Gabby repeated 'Mummummum' and he jokingly said 'Not dadadad!' She then repeated 'Dadadad'.

By the time Gabriella was 16m 3d:

> Said 'Pah' five times when I was referring to Pop. Looked at her family book, saying or repeating her version of the names: 'Ga' for herself, 'Mumum', 'Dadad' and 'Gogo' for Nicole.

Another occasion when Gabby was bursting to talk was when we went to the local theatre to see *We're Going on a Bear Hunt*.

> Gabby (17m 23d) was pretty much engaged throughout. She touched the puppets afterwards. She tried to say 'woof woof' and growled like a bear. She was almost telling the story.

Another motivation for expressing in language was at 18m 5m when playing with 3D noughts and crosses:

> At first she took some pieces off and put them back on, then began dropping them one by one into a box, saying 'Ma!' each time she dropped one in, as though counting. (This was frequently repeated with different objects.)

One day, I noted:

> New word today – 'Peppa' referring to Peppa Pig on TV. Gabby (22m 27d) said it several times this morning. Also says 'Kaka'. Evita told me she spoke to Gabby in Latvian yesterday and she replied with quite an emphatic 'Ja!'

Other new words noted were 'bubba' (for bubbles at 23m 5d) and 'pop' when stamping on bubbles at 23m 22d. She frequently said 'ma' (meaning 'more') and raised one finger when adding to a line of glass beads.

Links with Theory

It is generally accepted that children learn to understand language before expressing their ideas in language (Blackburn 2014). Blackburn also points out that, before children can talk about something in the absence of the object or some sort of concrete reminder, they need to have grasped the idea of 'object permanence' – that objects continue to exist even when we cannot see them (p.75). Drawing on a wide range of research, she also states that at 'around 15 months, words become free of context and a kind of language explosion marks a significant development in vocabulary' (p.74). However, there is a wide variation among individual children. I would say what we saw with Gabby at this point was a big increase in understanding and the wish to communicate, for example, 'bursting to tell the story of *We're Going on a Bear Hunt*'. She was living in a household where Latvian as well as English is spoken and, although her parents emphasized English as the main language spoken, Gabby may also be picking up the sounds necessary for speaking Latvian.

Reflections
What are the ways in which we can help children learn language?
Have you noted down when a child understands something for the first time?
What else might be significant about receptive or expressive language in the early years?

Repeated Patterns of Action/Schemas

Although I have been studying young children and, in particular, noticing their 'repeated patterns of action' or 'schemas' for over 30 years, this was my first opportunity during that time to spend so much time with a child so young. What surprised me most was that Gabriella was exploring a cluster of schemas from when she was quite young. I had not expected the learning through schemas to be as complex and also as unpredictable. Whenever we planned for an individual child at nursery, we noticed the cluster of schemas but assumed these accumulated with age and that is true to some extent. We saw in Chapter 1 that Gabriella gradually, through her actions, became more adept at, for example, 'grabbing objects' and then 'manipulating' them. Towards the end of that first year, she seemed to be noticing objects that 'rotate'. At that time, I used the language 'round and round' to support her knowledge of rotating. According to Athey (2007: 125), 'when the environment is supportive verbally, children become able to internalize successfully a range of actions'. So 'tuning in conceptually' is a helpful role for adults (Atherton and Nutbrown 2013).

When one first hears about schemas, it is not difficult to spot the patterns in children's play. However, my aim in this section is to take us a little further into understanding learning through schemas. Having trawled through a huge amount of data on Gabriel-la's second year, I find it significant when I notice what Athey calls:

- a 'functional dependence relationship'; that is, 'when children observe the effects of action on objects or material' (1990: 70)
- when children use one object to stand for another as in pretend play – these are referred to as 'symbolic representations' using 'actions, mark making and other graphic forms and speech' (Athey 2013: 9)
- when 'accommodations' are made; that is, when children 'come to know' or are able to do something that previously they struggled with.

Gabby's Cluster of Schemas

Across her second year, Gabby explored the following patterns:

- Enclosing: enclosing oneself, an object or space.
- Going through a boundary: causing oneself or some material to go through a boundary and emerge on the other side.
- Connecting: connecting themselves to objects and objects to each other.
- Trajectory: moving in or representing straight lines, arcs or curves.
- Rotating: turning, twisting or rolling oneself or objects in the environment around.
- Enveloping: enveloping, covering or surrounding oneself, an object or a space.
- Dabbing: making a stabbing trajectory movement, sometimes resulting in a mark.
- Twoness: being interested in and aware of two as a concept.
- Transporting: carrying objects or being carried from one place to another.
- Whole and parts: showing a concern for connecting objects into a whole, directly preceding the ability to conserve.
- On top: putting oneself or objects on top of other objects.
- One-to-one correspondence: placing objects or acting on objects or people in a one-to-one correspondence.
- Containing: putting materials or oneself inside an object which is capable of containing them.
- Inside: being interested in the inside space of a container and in going inside a space or container.

(Definitions from Arnold 1997)

There were numerous examples of each of these patterns, often repeated with different objects. Often, Gabby would seek out a **variable** to try out her latest action on, to see whether she got the same result. Towards the end of her first year, we saw Gabby co-ordinating containing and trajectory, for example by putting something in a box and moving it up and down until it fell out. Gabby (11m 23d) placed a ball inside a slinky and shook it. Here are further examples of Gabby seeking out variables. At 12m 22d:

> Played ball using little wooden ball . . . threw it up hallway in bathroom on tiled floor, then on bathmat. Went as far as front door. Rubbed it on coarse doormat (causing friction).

The effect would have been very different on the different surfaces:

> At Nicole's school, Gabby (15m 28d) is still going up the slope and coming down on her feet but also on her bottom.

The feel of coming down on her feet may have been quite different to coming down on her bottom. At 16m 14d, she:

> took magnetic letter off fridge door and tried it on hall wall. It fell off.

In this case, she discovered that the wall was different to the fridge.

> At a carer/child group, Gabby (17m 25d) played with sand. Filled a bucket not very effectively using a wooden spoon and then, much more effectively, with a scoop.

At our house:

> Gabby (19m 2d) put on Nicole's slippers and walked up and down the hall several times and into the kitchen, making more noise on the tiled floor in the kitchen.

So Gabby seemed to be noticing a different effect when walking on the different surfaces and was actually seeking that different effect.

A favourite aim of Gabby's at this time was to fasten (connect) the seatbelt on her highchair at our house. When she (20m 17d) was confident about fastening the belt while standing on the floor and facing her chair:

> Gabby indicated that she wanted to sit in her highchair and try to do up the fastener from that angle.

This was much trickier without the fastener in front of her at eye level, and definitely a new challenge she set herself. If we watch children carefully, they often set themselves challenges far in advance of what we may plan for their learning.

Finally, Gabby (21m 24d) seemed to be interested in the prepositions that described her actions – 'in front' and 'behind':

> Gabby got a small piece of dough and kept throwing it in front of her and behind her, several times and became quite excited. Went back to sand and used similar action with small amounts of sand.

It is obvious in these examples that Gabby was experimenting and looking for the different effects of her actions with different materials or in different circumstances, thereby adding to her knowledge of what happened when she carried out a particular action. Piaget (1980: 11) mentions this tendency:

> He varies them intentionally in order to study the results of these variations and thus gives himself over to true explorations . . .

Understanding Functional Dependency Relationships

According to Athey (2013: 9), when children understand what will happen as a result of their action, this demonstrates progression. There are several examples in the data where I could deduce that Gabby was aware of what would happen. Often, this involved something she had experimented with previously. At 12m 3d, she:

> noticed box with drawers, moved towards it and seemed to remember to put her finger through the small metal handle to open the drawer – did it two or three times . . . Later on, (she was) pleased to notice cloth book with loop at corner and carried it on her finger.

These actions involved knowledge of, in schema terms, 'enclosing' and 'going through a boundary'.

Pic 2.1 Going through loop on drawer

Gabby (12m 13d) shuffled along the hall to where there was a nightlight:

> When the light was switched on and the hall was reasonably dark, the light came on. Gabby immediately covered the appropriate spot (sensor) with her finger, making the light go off. She tried with one finger and then with her whole hand and both worked.

Here, she was using 'enveloping' to make the light go off. The fact that she tried her finger and then her whole hand may indicate that she was still at a stage of trying out what worked. Already mentioned in this chapter was her knowledge of the music centre at home when, at 14m 23d, she used a 'dab' movement on two specific buttons to play music. Similarly to this observation:

> I switched the standard lamp on and off once . . . Some time later, Gabby (17m 29d) noticed the red switch, went over and pressed it on and off several times, looking quite pleased with herself. She did not quite understand which part of the switch she needed to press each time so was using trial and error.

So, again, Gabby was still exploring how this worked rather than carrying out the action knowledgeably. A few weeks later, I noted:

> Gabby (19m 2d) played with the nightlight, switching it on and off several times. Then, as though a light went on in her head, she went to the standard lamp in the living room and switched that on and off several times.

Here, Gabby seems to be making connections between the switches. I would even say that this is evidence of her **thinking**, as she must have seen a similarity between the switches even though the standard lamp was in another room.

A much easier connection to make was when:

> Gabby (22m 16d) put on her sister's shoes and stomped around the room (she knew you had to emphasize steps to make sparkle happen).

These were the sorts of trainers that sparkle when you jump or land heavily on them. Gabby had observed her sister making them sparkle and imitated Nicole's actions.

Symbolic Representation

Athey (2013: 9) informs us that symbolic play is occurring when 'something is used to stand for something else'. This 're-playing' (Athey: 1990) of experiences can involve 'actions, mark making and other graphic forms and speech' (2013: 9). There are only a few instances in this second year where I noted that Gabriella engaged in symbolic play:

> Twice today, Gabby (14m 23d) seemed to pretend to be asleep – at the children's centre, lying on a beanbag, making a kind of 'ssh' snoring sound, then in the car, she did the same when cuddling a small teddy.

A couple of days later:

> I said something about 'asleep' and Gabby put her head to the side to feign sleep?

We were attending a group where Gabriella (15m 2d) spent most time with the dolls and cradle. As part of her play, she:

> fed doll with bottle several times . . . Brought funnel from water to dough, put bits of dough inside – later 'fed' doll with funnel.

This developed further when Gabby (15m 28d):

> also 'fed' doll and teddy with her drink and, for the first time, made a movement and sound with her mouth as she put it to their mouths. REALLY pretending.

Gabriella engaged in some of this early symbolic play with her sister, for example at 17m:

> At home, playing shops with Nicole, pressing buttons on cash-card machine and talking to customers using the microphone.

Obviously, this play was assisted by having a play shop and other resources, as well as her older sister as a more knowledgeable partner at home (Vygotsky 1986).

When Gabriella was 19m 11d, I bought a buggy and baby for playing with at our house and this prompted a great deal of symbolic play that became more apparent and complex as Gabby became older.

I also collected samples of Gabby's mark making from this time. There are numerous up/down and side-to-side marks (trajectories), some round and round (rotating or enclosing) but only one where Gabby (23m 25d) named her drawing 'Tiger'.

Pic 2.2 'A tiger'

Accommodations

According to Athey (2007: 7), 'knowledge consists of cognitive structures (schemas and concepts)'. We have all experienced the idea that 'the penny drops' when we adjust to some new learning. I looked for instances when Gabriella accommodated some new learning.

We saw in Chapter 1 that I made a family book for Gabby (8m 16d) and that, after showing it to her for the first time, I removed the names, laminated them and put Velcro on the book and on the back of each name so that Gabby could separate them from the book and connect them. She frequently separated the names from the book but it was months before she learned how to connect them.

> Today, Gabby (13m 15d) accommodated to the idea of putting the names on the Velcro bit of each page. Previously she tried putting them anywhere. She knew what she'd done and clapped and looked very pleased.

The threshold from the kitchen to conservatory consists of a 3-inch (7cm) sill to step over. Gabby negotiated this carefully from when she was first mobile. When she was 14m 15d, I noticed her negotiating this sill with ease or 'without thinking', as I noted at the time. This accommodation had occurred without me noticing.

Another piece of learning that involved a long apprenticeship was dressing her toys and herself. She was very determined to understand how to do this. We were at the Growing Together group when:

> Gabby (14m 26d) took the cardigan off a doll and several times placed the cardigan on top of the doll (I think she wants to take it off ('separate') and put back on ('connect')).

And at home:

> Gabby (15m 8d) took clothes off babies (dolls) and tried to put them back on.

At 15m 23d:

> At Growing Together again – (she was) attracted by babies. Came to me with doll and nappy. Tends to put clothes on top of doll.

At 16m 3d at our home, she was:

> interested in taking off and putting on Teddy Tim's trousers. Put them on top. . . (then comes a partial accommodation. . .) Put her arm through trouser leg and walked around with it like that, looking quite pleased.

At this point, I think Gabby was realizing that 'on top' was different to 'going through' and being 'inside' a garment. Gabriella continued exploring this 'going through a boundary' schema in different ways and also watched carefully when I put nappies on babies or got them dressed. When she was 17m 18d at Growing Together, she:

> Liked putting large dolly's knickers on her own leg – only managed one leg through but made movements to suggest she knew the other leg should 'go through'. Similarly, with doll's cardigan although it was much too small.

Gabriella continued to explore 'going through' with lots of other resources, including pastry cutters, slats in a ladder, post box and so on, until one day at her home:

> Gabby (22m 20d) spent ages in the hall. We went to see what she was doing. She had put on Nicole's pyjama bottoms – on both legs properly but not pulled up to waist. She was very pleased with herself.

At this point, I deduced that Gabby had accommodated the idea that the limbs need to 'go through' the arms and legs of clothing items to get dressed, though, at some level, she had experienced this when she was dressed by others.

Another long apprenticeship Gabby served this year, which I have mentioned already, was learning to fasten the seatbelt on her highchair. The fastener was one of those 'childproof' three-way fasteners. Each of the sides had to be inserted into the middle and it was tricky even for adults. Gabby (12m 22d) began by putting the connectors close to each other, having no real concept of how it connected. Gabby persevered and practised almost every day she was at our house until she mastered fastening it at 20m 16d (Arnold 2014).

Links with Theory

I have tried to get to the heart of learning by highlighting the progress Gabby made during this period. Noticing when Gabby knew what would happen as a result of her actions (functional dependency relations) is important (Athey 1990: 70), although it is not set in stone, as may have been indicated in stage theory, much of which has been refuted. There is a difference between carrying out an action *to find out* the result and carrying out an action when you *know* what will happen. The latter shows progress. It is not only children who discover how something works by experimenting. We do this throughout our lives but older people have the advantages of greater experience and language abilities, so some processes can be explained to us. However, we still discover, practise and master how to do things. Athey (2007: 113), in her chapter 'From action to thought', uses the terms 'motor **level**', 'symbolic representational **level**' and 'thought **level**', which puts me in mind of a simple hierarchical structure. I prefer to think of these actions as different 'ways' children explore schemas because they are not strictly hierarchical (Arnold 2013: 173).

Symbolic representation becomes prevalent around the age of 2 years and, therefore, is developmental. At first, the child uses something quite similar to the real object; for example, when Gabby put a remote control to her ear and said 'Hello'. Gradually, the symbol becomes more detached. The important aspect is that children are drawing on their lived experience, in effect 're-playing' an experience (Athey: 2007: 53). In terms of what we offer children, Athey suggests 'feeding' schemas and accompanying children's actions with language in order to help them become consciously aware of their 'doing' (1990, 2007).

Reflections

Are you spotting repeated patterns/schemas and not sure where to go from there?

What sorts of resources could you offer to support a child exploring, for example, connecting?

How might your language contribute to the learning?

What about stories that might tune in conceptually?

SUMMARY

This chapter charted Gabriella's development and learning during her second year. The most important and frequently reported were data on her:

- receptive and expressive language development
- repeated actions/schemas explored.

Gabby explored the following cluster of schemas in different ways during this year:

- Enclosing
- Going through a boundary
- Connecting
- Trajectory
- Rotating
- Enveloping
- Dab
- Twoness
- Transporting
- Whole and parts
- On top
- One-to-one correspondence
- Containing
- Inside.

As far as pedagogy is concerned:

Intent	Implementation	Impact
Conducting conversations through gesture	Noticing what Gabby means and responding, e.g. with blowing bubbles	Gabby squeals with excitement
Extending her world (knowledge and understanding)	Taking Gabby to see the ducks	She mirrors the actions of the ducks
Extending her world (physical development)	Taking Gabby to a park	Chuffedness when she masters steps and slide
Supporting Gabby's language and understanding	Looking at picture books and taking her to the theatre	She conducts conversations through gesture
Extending her world (music)	Playing a variety of music to her	She listens and reacts through actions including clapping

(continued)

(*continued*)

Intent	Implementation	Impact
Supporting Gabby to understand reasons for a delay etc.	Explaining to her and giving her time to think	She thinks about it and agrees
Identifying Gabby's interest in rotating	Using language to match her interest	She repeats and adopts on other similar relevant occasions
Helping Gabby to understand where her parents and sister are	Looking at family book and talking about family	Her involvement in and use of her version of names and holding in mind her family when they are not present
'Feeding' schemas	Offering variables and supporting Gabby to seek out variables	Assimilations and accommodations, e.g. applying 'ra ra' to other objects that rotate
Extending learning whenever Gabby shows an interest	Being patient and following her lead	Accommodation, e.g. she learns to fasten a 'childproof' seatbelt

3   From 2 to 3 Years

Changes were afoot for Gabriella during this year. Her grandparents from Latvia visited for a couple of weeks just after her second birthday, Gabby started attending nursery part-time and my husband and I visited our younger daughter in Australia twice during that year, firstly for two weeks and later on for six weeks.

Reading through the diary, I noticed that Gabby's world seemed to expand and she responded much of the time by taking control of what we did and by expressing a range of emotions to communicate her feelings.

Her physical and intellectual development continued at a pace and her language became much more fluent and joined up. So the themes emerging for Gabby's third year are:

- Autonomy
- Emotions
- Physical, intellectual and language development.

Autonomy

'Autonomy' is defined as 'independence' or 'self-government', and this very much conveys what we saw happening with Gabby during this year. By now, Gabby seemed to know about the range of experiences we could offer and she was quick to opt for a particular action. For example:

> Went to town to the bank – Gabby (24m) liked putting the money in the machine to get a parking ticket – it was 60p – she put in 50p and immediately pressed the green button and then had to put another 10p in.

During that year, she became adept at getting the ticket and also taking out money at the bank. A more frequent choice she made when with us was *where* we would go. When she was 2y 3m 5d, I asked Gabby:

> 'Would you like to go and see Cathy (at Adult/Infant Drop-in)?'
>
> 'No.'
>
> 'Would you like to go to Pen Green?'
>
> 'No.'
>
> 'We can't go to the park as it's misty and damp.'
>
> Finally, Gabby said 'Yes' to the library.

These were frequent conversations in which we offered some choices and, occasionally, a rationale about why a trip to the park (her favourite) was not viable. Gabby also loved being in control of materials. For example, when we were at a drop-in group:

> Gabby (2y 3m 14d) was 'feeding' a baby doll – Cathy put wet wipes out – Gabby loved wiping baby's face, hands, feet and legs and then putting the wipe in the bin. She absolutely loved the freedom of getting wet wipes, using them on baby and then throwing them away – the whole sequence of actions.

Going out for lunch became quite a regular occurrence. Once, when we went into town:

> I had a latte and Gabby (2y 3m 19d) had milkshake. I ordered bacon and egg with toast and gave Gabby some egg and toast. She was really good – kept lifting the milkshake down from the table so she could drink it and would not let me help. Ate up all the egg and some of the toast. (I was so focused on Gabby that I forgot to pay and the owner of the café had to chase after us!)

Sometimes, Gabriella watched other children doing something she had not quite mastered yet and that seemed to make her more determined to master those actions. For example, in the soft-play room:

> From sitting on the edge of the ballpool, Gabby (2y 3m 27d) slid in, holding Pop's hand, and then saw other children sliding in without help, so she slid in without help about six times.

Gabriella continued dressing herself and became toilet trained and, one day when I visited her home:

> Gabby (2y 6m 30d) and her mum were dancing with the Wii. Gabby concentrated on copying the movements on the screen. She had a remote control in her hand with no batteries but her mum had the actual remote. Gabby kept saying 'It's annoying' when the movement on screen did not respond to her remote ('annoying' is her new word).

We prepared Gabriella well for our six-week trip to Australia, and the day before setting off we went to town to buy a new suitcase:

> Gabby (2y 7m 12d) pushed the large suitcase from the store to the car park. She did not want us to help.

We FaceTimed while we were away and this seemed to ease the transition from being together to being apart and then back together again. On our return, it was Easter Sunday and I noted:

> Gabby (2y 9m 25d) enjoyed using her scooter, following Nicole. She has mastered scooting with one foot on the scooter and propelling with the other foot on the ground. Not yet putting both feet on the scooter to coast along.

Around this time, Gabriella was practising using scissors and also cutting her food with a knife. I tried to help by setting up strips of paper on a line so that she could practise cutting with scissors. I noted:

> Gabby (2y 10m 3d) practised cutting the suspended strips of paper. She found it totally involving but very hard work.
>
> Went to Asda with Gabby (2y 10m 20d) and bought playdough. Then we went to The Range for a blunt knife so that she could practise cutting.
>
> Looked after Gabby (2y 11m 22d) all day . . . she was pleased to see me, confident and very chatty. After being out all morning, Gabby said 'I want to go to the park'.

This was a frequent occurrence, as there is a small park at the end of our road.

> I said 'OK', then she said 'Not that *little* park'. . . I asked 'Where?' She said 'Wicksteed Park' (which is 7 miles away in the next town). I said we could go after lunch and she was happy with that.

Links with Theory

Erik Erikson identified eight stages in a child's psychosocial development. He identified the second stage in early childhood as being a time when 'children develop a greater sense of personal control' (Cherry 2020). According to Erikson, gaining more control results in children feeling 'secure' and 'confident'. Gabriella had a real drive at this time to be more independent but we had to support her in her quest for independence. Erskine (2019: 24) points out that 'the quality of autonomy that children develop depends on their parents' ability to grant autonomy with dignity and a sense of personal independence'. So, I would deduce that we also have a role to play in children gaining independence. Côté-Lecaldare et al. (2016) talk about supporting the development of autonomy in young children by 'offering choices and encouraging initiatives, acknowledging the child's feelings and perspective, and providing rationales and explanations for requests' (p.822). Recent thinking also attributes 'agency' to children who are given autonomy. Agency can be defined as 'children's capacity to make a difference' (Oswell 2013: 6). So, rather than regarding adults as the source of everything young children need to learn, the young children themselves can be seen as contributors and constructors of knowledge. I think this is largely how we tried to regard Gabby.

Reflections

Are you aware of when the children you work with are striving for independence?
In what ways can you support their quest for autonomy?
What sorts of boundaries might you need to set?

Emotions

Gabriella experienced some very happy and settled times during this year, as well as some challenges. Just after her second birthday, her Opi (Latvian for Grandad) and his wife Irina visited for two weeks. They had been regularly video calling and Gabby was really pleased to meet them for the first time. They visited us twice, the first time to meet us and the second time for all of us to have a meal together. On both occasions, the weather was lovely and we sat in the garden. Gabby seemed really settled:

> Gabby (2y 11d) pushed the baby (doll) and buggy up and down the garden path, fed 'baby' then played blowing bubbles in the garden. She brought her musical counting book outside and danced to the music. We all applauded.

Gabby seemed to know that she had an appreciative audience.

Several entries in the diary indicate that, at this time, Gabby got upset whenever we had to leave any of the parks we frequented. This got better during the year when we began saying 'Bye-bye park' and 'We'll come back another day'. It seemed that Gabby learned to understand why we had to leave and to trust that we would visit the park again.

Just before we went to Australia for the first time during that year, I noted how confident Gabby was when accompanied by her sister:

> One day, I had to pop into the Pen Green Research Base to say that I could not attend a meeting today. The two girls were delightful – Gabby (2y 1m 14d) was much more confident along-side Nicole – smiling and laughing, hiccupping, waving and saying 'Bye'. We went to Wicksteed Park from there. Gabby said 'Yeh!' in anticipation.

Naturally, there were times when the two girls argued:

> Gabby (2y 1m 7m) was distraught when I got to their house – something to do with Nicole having marbles. First, Evita was comforting her, then Paul. She pushed me away at first. Paul was saying 'We love you' and holding her. When it was time for us to go, she somehow came out of it. She cuddled Teddy Tom in the car.

After our two weeks in Australia visiting our new-born granddaughter, Anya, Gabby was a bit shy and reserved with me at first. On our first day together, we did some of the usual things, visiting the Adult/Infant Drop-in and playing there. However, at home, after a sleep, Gabriella got very upset as she did not want to eat anything from her lunchbox (which her mum prepared each day). I noted:

> Gabby (2y 2m 2d) spent the next 35 minutes crying very loudly. Her nose was running and she was dribbling. She would not allow me or Pop to comfort her. I kept wiping her face and saying 'You are very cross and sad'. Nothing seemed to work. Eventually Pop went and got bubbles and, somehow, that distracted her. She spent the next 30 minutes blowing bubbles, also ate some fruit. She took the bubbles home with her.

It is only in retrospect that I have puzzled over this and wondered whether Gabby needed to express her sadness at our previous absence.

Starting Nursery

Gabby's next big challenge was starting nursery at 2y 3m 19d. This was in the October and we reasoned that Gabby would be well settled by the end of January when Pop and I were going to Australia for six weeks and the family might require extra childcare hours to cover their work patterns. I took her on her first day. The practice is for parents or carers to stay in or around the nursery for the first two weeks or until a child is settled. I noted that it was 'harder for me than it was for Gabby'.

All went well until Gabby 'tripped over' and 'cried very loudly'. I felt this was a release of tension following conversations about being 'a big girl' and 'starting nursery'. I noted:

> Gabby seemed much better after a good cry. I didn't offer her her dummy and she didn't ask.

Subsequently, Gabby would usually place her special teddy (Lacitis) and dummy in her communication box at nursery so that she could access them when she needed them. Ten days after starting nursery, I noticed a new pattern in her play:

> We were playing in the lobby of Growing Together. Gabby (2y 3m 29d) was going up the steps and down the slope. She held a small pig, then let the pig roll down the slope. Also threw the pig over the side – I've not seen her do this kind of throwing or dropping for ages – does it link with starting nursery and letting attachment figures go? Also placed animal figures on top several times.

Links with Theory

Susan Isaacs (1952:72) cited an observation made by Freud of 'a boy of eighteen months' who was well behaved and seemed to cope well with his separation from his mother, but developed a game of 'throwing small objects into the corner of the room or under the bed . . . he would say 'o-o-o-h' which his mother thought meant "gone away"'. I, too, have noticed children symbolizing separation in different ways in their play (documented in Arnold and the Pen Green Team 2010). It may be notable that Gabby also placed some animals 'on top'. Maybe she or some of the other children felt 'on top' at this time.

Gaining Satisfaction from Challenges

Gabby loved to engage in physical play at this time. If we could go to a park, she was very happy and constantly challenged herself. If we could not go to a park because of the weather, we often went to indoor soft-play areas where there was climbing equipment. On one of those occasions, we took Gabby (2y 4m 2d) to Kids Play at Kettering. After trying out several vehicles, small slides and climbing equipment, she accessed the biggest slide:

> Pop slid down alongside her three times. There were 27 steps up to the top of the slide and, after three turns, Pop was exhausted. Gabriella still started climbing up the steps – I was scared but felt I had to follow. Gabby and I came down together three times. She cried when we left.

Understanding How Others are Feeling

The following day, we were looking at video on my phone of Gabby and Pop coming down the big slide and then Gabby and I coming down the slide.

> Gabby looked serious and said 'Care' and, again, 'care'. I didn't click at first and then I said 'Scared?' She nodded and said 'Mop'. I agreed that 'Mop was scared' and she pointed at herself and said 'Me' and shook her head. [Wow! That's some understanding from a 2-year-old!]

Links with Theory

My initial thought was that Gabby was developing 'Theory of Mind' (TOM), described by Jenvey and Newton as the idea that 'cognitive capacities develop and enable children to understand that they themselves and others have thoughts, feelings, beliefs and intentions' (2015: 164). Gabby clearly expressed the idea that I felt differently than her during this experience, which, I thought, indicated some degree of empathy. I reasoned that she had felt scared at some time and could, therefore, see and understand that I was scared. Many of the studies on TOM involve experimental studies and these are very different to a naturalistic study such as this study. These experimental studies tend to use 'false belief' tasks and state that TOM develops between 3 and 5 years of age (Jenvey and Newton 2015: 168).

Trevarthen et al. (2018b: 311) disagree with the idea that TOM is learned but state that children possess 'an 'innate sympathy', a creative feeling for relating that seeks to complement and contribute to what other human beings experience'. This would indicate a biological ability to understand others, but I still think that experiences count too, as they do with most abilities.

A Couple of 'Wobbles'

Shortly after this, Evita was away for three nights. Gabriella (2y 4m 15d) cried each morning. We thought this was OK as she was merely expressing her sadness, rather like her cousin, Harry, when his mum took him and his sister on their first holiday without their dad (Arnold 2003). During that weekend, I offered to look after Nicole while Paul was taking Gabby for her flu jab, as Nicole hates needles. However, we changed our plans when we realized how much Gabby needed her sister for security when her mum was away, so we all had a nice day together. On the Sunday, they were at our house:

> At one point, Gabby came and lay on me with me holding her for a good five minutes or so (reminded me of what she'd done after missing me, only now she was missing Mummy).

About 10 days after this, after being unwell and missing nursery for a few days, Gabriella had a real 'wobble' and did not want to stay at nursery. The first time it happened, she was 2y 4m 26d, and I took her home rather than leaving her upset. The next couple of sessions, either Paul or I stayed with her at nursery to try to settle her again. Around this time, I noticed that:

> when Gabby was looking at photos on my phone, she 'whizzed' past the photos taken at nursery.

Her family worker, Sam, came for a home visit. The next day, Evita took her to nursery and explained to her that 'Mummy and Daddy have to go to work, Nicole has to go to school and nursery is your work'. Although Evita had to leave her crying the first couple of days, we were able to ring up and check she had settled shortly after. Gradually, when Gabriella was more settled, Paul or I could once more take her to nursery. In discussion, we realized it was partly our issue with separation (see *Links with Theory* below) (Arnold et al. 2018). I noted, when Gabby was 2y 6m 7d, that she was 'much happier going to nursery now' and a couple of weeks later that 'we looked at Gabriella's *Going to Nursery* book'.

Pic 3.1 *Going to Nursery* book

This seemed to be a sign of her being much more settled and wanting to talk about nursery and the people she knew from nursery.

Links with Theory

Gabriella's sadness when her mother was away for three nights was understandable and, in a way, she was able to handle it by relying on her sister for security. She also, unusually, 'lay on me' for comfort. This is similar to what Harry learned to do when he was reunited with his mother or father after an absence (Arnold 2003). Later on, Harry learned to seek this sort of comfort in advance of a planned separation. This all links to 'attachment' theory and 'attachment figures' and Gabriella was using 'subordinate attachment figures' for security (her sister, father and me) (Bowlby 1997: 205).

Our reluctance to leave Gabby at nursery when she was unsettled goes all the way back to our experience of a forced separation when Paul was 6 months old and my sister was involved in a serious car accident. Although it was over 40 years ago, we found we still both felt reluctant to relive the pain of that earlier separation. In psychoanalytic circles, this would be referred to as 'Ghosts in the Nursery' (Fraiberg et al. 2003).

Getting a 'Big Girl's' Bed

Although Evita and Paul reported that Gabby (2y 6m 28d) was excited about going into a bed, what we did not expect was her reaction to the departure of her cot. I noted:

> Gabriella's big girl bed arrived today. Paul told me she cried for about an hour yesterday when two ladies came to pick up her cot. She was very angry, kicking Paul. Although she knew she was going to get a bed, she did not realize that her cot would go.

The following day, Evita told me:

> In the morning, Gabby sat on her new bed with her hands clasped in front of her chest and said 'I loved my cot'.

Pic 3.2 Gabby standing up in her beloved cot

Links with Theory

Gabby's unexpected 'loss' of her cot also resonated with 'attachment' to a loved object and, in this case, after her immediate outburst, she was able to articulate to her mum why she felt sad and angry: 'I loved my cot'.

Continuing to Show a Range of Emotions

During this time, Gabriella continued to show great pleasure (chuffedness) and also anger when things she wanted to do were considered unsafe for her. A notable example:

> When we dropped Nicole at school, Gabriella (2y 7m 1d) wanted to walk on the wall (as she does frequently) but it was wet so Evita said 'No' as it was dangerous. Gabby was furious and screamed from then till we almost reached her mum's work. Evita offered her her dummy, which she threw down, and screamed 'Dummies are for babies!' Eventually, she calmed down and kissed her mum, goodbye, asking her regular question 'No lipstick?' Evita replied 'No lipstick'.

Soon after this, we went to Australia for six weeks. By now, Gabriella seemed to have a better understanding that we were going away but would return. She was very pleased to see us when we came back and to revisit all of her regular play at our home.

Gabby had one more small 'wobble' when her parents and family worker were discussing whether it was time for her to move into the big nursery at Easter. It was not discussed directly with Gabriella but we think she just sensed that changes might be afoot. They decided it would be better to wait until the summer when Gabby would be 3 years old, by which time she had gained a lot more confidence and had independently, alongside her friends, accessed the area she would be moving to.

Links with Theory

Gabby's wish to walk on the wall was thwarted by her mum, who felt it dangerous when it was wet. Again, Gabby's outburst was spontaneous and, according to Dunn and Munn (1987), very common between young children and parents who set them boundaries.

Reflections

Think about whether you can tolerate a range of emotions displayed by young children.

What sorts of plans do you put in place to prepare a child for a change or transition?
How can you help a child to express their emotions?

Physical, Intellectual and Language Development

Many of the examples above relate to physical, intellectual and language development so, in this section, I will just give a few examples of how Gabby was progressing in those specific areas.

Physical Development

A couple of days after her second birthday, Gabriella was watching their rabbit, Fluffy, jump around in his cage. She began jumping on the decking and, for I think for the first time, both feet left the ground at once.

As I have mentioned, we made frequent visits to parks and soft-play areas, where Gabby could challenge herself physically. She was relentless in practising a skill in every way she could think of. One example:

We went to Mini Mischiefs (indoor play centre). Gabby (2y 7m 1d) went on the slide 21 times, and then went down on her tummy on her 23rd, 25th, 26th, 27th, 28th times, on her bottom with tongue out on her 30th and 31st times and alongside me (she invited me by saying 'Come with me') on her 34th, 35th and 36th times.

We went to a small soft room at our local children's centre at least once a week and Gabriella gradually mastered all the equipment on offer:

Gabby (2y 7m 10d) had a great time today – firstly jumping high on the trampoline and walking around the edge, then going up steps, down slope, through tunnel and into ball pool. At first, she asked me to help her climb out of the ball pool but, gradually, she mastered getting out by herself and then repeated this journey several times. Sometimes she walked along the edge of the ball pool and sometimes climbed on top of cylinder and, once or twice, slid down from there to the floor.

One thing that fascinated her, which was pictured in a book she often looked at but she could not yet do, was a handstand. Each time Gabby saw the picture she had another try, usually facing forward with both hands on the floor and one leg in the air.

Intellectual Development

Gabriella continued to explore and co-ordinate schemas, adding to her repertoire. She repeated her actions frequently using the same, similar and sometimes different resources. This was the year when she became more socially aware. She had friends at nursery and was also a lot more open to playing with other children in the soft room and at the drop-in groups we attended regularly. I could write a whole book on the data gathered this year. However, for the purposes of this chapter I will focus on some of the concepts Gabby was developing. We can think of schemas as 'partial concepts' and at this stage it was possible to identify some of the concepts she was interested in and developing through her cluster of schemas:

Number Sense

We are surrounded by numbers that denote ages, house numbers, phone numbers, time and a host of other meanings, which young children have to unravel. Children can learn to count by rote without a real understanding of what is signified by the sequence of numbers. However, Gelman and Gallistel (1986) produced a set of principles that show what children need to understand in order to fully understand counting:

1 The order of the numbers is fixed.
2 You must match one number name to one object.
3 The last number is the number of objects in the set.
4 You can count in any order – right to left or left to right, as long as each object is only counted once.
5 The arrangement of the objects does not matter – they can be spread out or put close together (explorations of this with objects leads to an understanding of 'conservation' of number).

The schemas that young children explore from an early age seem to help them establish some of this learning, for example 'lines and trajectories' establish an order going from less to more, as well as the 'form' of words and sentences; playing with making a 'one-to-one correspondence' contributes to counting each object only once; 'transporting' objects and arranging them in different ways contributes to the feel of 'less and more' or 'few and many', and also enables children to realize that the amount does not change when items are spread out or close together as long as long as nothing is taken away or added ('conservation of amount').

When Piaget was carrying out his research with young children, the children were often judged as 'deficit' but Chris Athey, in extending Piaget's work, was interested in what young children 'can do' (1990) and this is the approach I intend to take.

Gabriella's enduring interest in going up steps and down slides (exploring a 'trajectory' schema) prompted us to often count the steps out loud. She was experiencing the slope at the same time as the increasing height as she went up the steps in a 'one-to-one correspondence'. Gabby started at the lowest rung or step and moved up to the highest rung or step mirroring counting in action.

Gabby frequently played with fridge magnets both at home and at our house, and with glass beads at our house. The glass beads were in a bowl in the conservatory.

> Gabby (1y 11m 22d) carried beads, two or three at a time, to the outside table. As she put beads on the table, she made sounds as though counting. She put 37 beads in all on the table and left them there, roughly in a long line. They looked quite different.

Here, she was learning through her body how she could transform the look of 37 beads that were together in a bowl by 'transporting' them and arranging them differently.

> Gabby (2y 1m 11d) wanted the Snakes and Ladders (game) out. It was only the second time we had looked at them so I was interested in what she would do. Wasn't very interested in the die but took each counter out and moved across the board saying 'One . . . two', 'Two . . . one'. So she knew the game involved moving a counter and counting, although her counting was limited.

Gabby (2y 3m 1d) seemed to be understanding the concept of 'two-ness' when:

> we were in the bathroom. Gabby pointed at the taps and said 'Two'. I said 'And you've got two feet'. She lifted her top, pointed at her nipples and said 'Two', showing that she was noticing pairs of objects and possibly symmetry . . .
>
> Gabby (2y 3m 19d) was playing with Snakes and Ladders: 'Thought Gabby said 'One, two, three, four''.

Three months later:

> Gabby (2y 6m 19d) and Nicole played hide and seek. Gabby covered her eyes and counted from one to seven correctly first time. She understood about taking turns and the sequence of actions. When she counted too quickly, her mum said 'You need to count to ten'. Gabby said 'ten' and immediately wanted to go and find Nicole'.

Gabby often played with several dice and began matching amounts so, for example:

> Gabby (2y 7m 12d) lined her five dice up, matching the number of dots on each, firstly with fives, then ones, then twos.

Pic 3.3 Gabby lined up the dice, matching the number of dots

Seriation

'Seriation' is defined by Gruber and Voneche (1977: 359) as 'arranging a collection of things systematically with regard to some dimension along which they differ, for example, in order of size or desirability'. We noticed Gabriella showing an interest in comparing objects. I noted:

> Gabby (2y 5m 14d) is using lots of 'big/small', 'old/new'. Says 'new car seat' every time we get in the car. Also had 'new' leggings and top and 'new' teddy. . .

A few days later, at the boating lake park, Gabby referred to going on the 'baby slide' and 'big slide'. Athey (2007: 167) explains that, until a child acquires seriation, she uses 'absolute size notions such as "I am big. You are little"' and that these terms 'gradually become more differentiated, e.g. "I am bigger than you"'.

Gabby gradually used comparative terms. When she was 2y 10m 20d, I was pushing her on the swing at the park at the end of street, when she said:

> 'I want to go *as high as* that tree', pointing at a Lombardy poplar behind me.

This process culminated in the following, which I have coined a 'seriating game':

> I had brought playdough, rolling pin, flower-shaped cutters and a knife. Gabby (2y 11m 11d) turned this into a seriating game, arranging the flower cutters as follows:
>
> - Very little one – Anya (youngest/smallest in family).
> - Next in size (red) – Gabriella (favourite colour and second youngest/smallest in family).
> - Next in size (purple) – Mop (my favourite colour but a deviation in size and age).
> - Next in size (pink) – Nicole (favourite colour and next in size and age to Gabriella).
> - Next in size (orange) – Harry (next in age to Nicole).
> - Next in size (green) – Georgia (my eldest grandchild).
>
> Gabby appeared to be using two criteria to order the seriated cutters – size and person's favourite colour.

Gabriella (2y 11m 28d) repeated this game a couple of weeks later. This time, she swapped Harry and Georgia around, possibly because Harry is taller than Georgia, although he is a couple of years younger.

Pic 3.4 Gabby lined up the cutters in size order

Classifying

As well as comparing and seriating, Gabriella (2y 10m 13d) began grouping objects, firstly physically and then in her thinking:

> When I mentioned 'handstands', Gabby wanted to get her book, *The Baby's Catalogue*, where the handstand is pictured – she mentioned that Anya has the same book but that Gabby's has a red sticker on the front (to denote the '30th Anniversary Edition'). Looked at *Slinki Malinki* and Gabby pointed out that Nicole has *Scarface Claw* and repeatedly said she likes *Hairy Maclary* (all three books are in the same genre and by the same author!)

As well as grouping the dice according to the dots (as described above):

> We were getting into my car when Gabby (2y 11m 22d) recognized the car next to mine as being 'like Daddy's' (same make and colour).

Language Development

You can see from many of the communications above that Gabriella was communicating well. She seemed to go from single-word communications to two words to whole sentences. For a while, she could not pronounce 's' and used 'f' instead. So, when she first started nursery, she referred to her worker as 'Fam' (Sam). This resulted in a funny situation one day. Evita and I were standing up, talking to each other. Gabriella was sitting on the floor between us. Suddenly, our conversation was interrupted by Gabby proclaiming at the top of her voice 'Fock off!!' Her mother looked embarrassed and immediately said 'We don't use that language'. We both looked down and laughed as we saw that Gabby was proclaiming that she had managed to take her 'sock off'!

When analysing all Gabby's new language, I noted that she used full sentences from around 2y 6m, often to get her own needs or wants met. For example, at 2y 7m 8d, she said: 'I want to paint', expanding her reasoning by 2y 10m 6d, when she said: 'I want to go to the pet shop. My Daddy takes me to the pet shop'. At 2y 10m 20d, she added a causal clause: 'The American swing's gone because it was broken'. As mentioned earlier, Gabby (2y 11m 28d) also made comparisons, for example, at Fermyn Woods, when she said: 'They're my favourite swings'. Gabby frequently asked questions and we noticed, in retrospect, that much of her emerging language was linked to her schematic concerns (see Arnold 2018 for more on this topic). There was also proof that Gabby (2y 10m 13d) was picking up regional language use when Gabby said: 'It's my shot now' (this is the term a person from Corby would use, rather than 'my turn').

Links with Theory

Current research on 'embodied cognition' supports the view that we learn through our bodies and that body and brain are not two separate systems as was once thought. Thelen (2008: 101) explains: 'To say that cognition is *embodied* means that it arises from bodily interactions with the world and is continually meshed with them'. Thelen argues that 'the line between what is perception, action and cognition is very hard to draw' (2008: 110). Her theory is supported not only by Athey and Piaget's idea that our 'actions become our thoughts' but by researchers studying metaphor, who point out that much, if not all, of our metaphorical language is rooted in earlier actions (Johnson: 2008). As we progress through this book, it will become apparent that Gabriella's early actions become part of her language and thinking.

Athey, following Piaget's research, stated that young children make three major accommodations: seriation, classification and conservation (Athey 2004). A few of the observations above show that Gabby was working on all three of these concepts.

> **Reflections**
>
> How important do you think it is to record children's physical explorations?
>
> What are some of the ways we can support children's language development?
>
> Are you aware of links between language and schemas?
>
> What do you think about the idea that actions become thinking?

SUMMARY

This chapter charted Gabriella's third year. What was most important to her were:

* autonomy – she desperately wanted to do things for herself
* emotions – these seemed raw but, with her language developing, Gabby was beginning to express her feelings in words and to understand how others were feeling.

Alongside these prominent themes, Gabriella was continuing to develop:

* physically, intellectually and with language – although these were split into separate areas, each were closely intertwined.

The pedagogy we adopted seemed more deliberate during this year:

Intent	Implementation	Impact
Offering choices/ following her lead	Listening and acting on what she wanted to do whenever possible or explaining why not if it is not possible	Gabby's sense of self is strong. She values herself and feels valued
Accepting and helping her to articulate her feelings	Using the language of emotions ('sad', 'angry', 'happy') and remaining calm when she was uncontrollably angry	She begins to understand herself and others a little, e.g. her observation of me being scared on big slide

(continued)

(*continued*)

Intent	Implementation	Impact
Preparing her for our extended holidays in Australia	Talking about proposed trip, looking at photos and video of family in Australia and FaceTiming while we were away	She begins to understand we were going away but would come back and that it was OK to feel sad
Expanding her language through stories	Consciously using verbs as well as nouns when looking at picture books	She gains a wider experience through picture and story books
Making books about Gabby's family and experiences to engage her further	As well as her 'Family Book', she could share other suitable books, e.g. *I Want My Mum* and *Going to Nursery*	She is able to reflect on her own experiences
Support her language development and offer a different experience	Attending singing and rhyme time groups weekly	She learns new rhymes and enjoys singing alongside other children and adults
Widening her experience	Going to parks and soft-play areas	She learns to challenge herself physically
Tuning in 'conceptually'	Counting the steps at the park or play area	She learns some aspects of counting
Offering practice in other skills she was learning	Setting up strips of paper for Gabby to practise cutting	She becomes more adept at cutting
Offering practice in cutting with a knife	Bought playdough, blunt knife and baking set	She becomes skilled at cutting her food
Offering language to explain concepts	When she is trying out magnets on different surfaces, offering language, e.g. 'This is metal' and 'This is not metal'	She begins to understand the concept of magnetism

4 From 3 to 4 Years

This was the year when peer relationships became important to Gabriella. It was also when she moved into the 'big' nursery – the 'pre-school' year, as it is currently called in England, and, when role play reigned. The following themes emerged from the data gathered:

- Relationships/friendships
- Role play
- Schemas
- New language
- Science, technology and mathematical development
- Anomalies.

Relationships/Friendships

A week or two before her third birthday, Gabby lost her precious teddy (Lacitis). Despite searching, her parents could not find him, so asked us to buy her the same teddy for her birthday to replace her lost 'friend'. We agreed and I was quite nervous on her birthday:

> Gabriella was thrilled and immediately took to Teddy, cuddling him and not wanting to be separated from him.

It was good that Gabby connected with this new teddy as, a couple of weeks later, she gave up her dummy, very much in negotiation with her mum. We did notice her missing her mum a bit more than usual in the days immediately after but, all in all, she coped well.

Pic 4.1 Teddy (Lacitis)

Her best friend from the Nest (the nursery area for children from 9 months to around 3 years) had moved into the Den (the 'big' nursery) which adjoined the Nest, and I noted:

Gabby (3y 1m 6d) spent all morning in the Den with her friend.

The idea was that children could choose to move into the adjacent space for periods of time when they felt confident to do so. A few days later, Gabby went to nursery reluctantly, but settled when another friend arrived. When I picked her up, she told me, 'I have two friends'. I said, 'What about a little boy who is a family friend?' Gabby said 'Three friends!'

Her cousin, Anya, came to visit from Australia when Gabby was 3y 2m. Gabby was very interested in her and, because she is 2 years younger than Gabby, also quite protective of her. During the following year, Gabby and Anya interacted on Face-Time but they did not really get to know each other until Anya's family moved back to the UK and they were able to spend extended time together. Following on from this visit, Gabby's family went to Cornwall on holiday and, after their holiday, Gabby started attending the 'big' nursery. Her family worker, Shelley, chosen by her parents, visited the family at home prior to the move and we settled her in again, as we had done initially. Gabby settled well until one day:

> Gabby (3y 3m 4d) didn't want to go to nursery today but, when Shelley mentioned having nail varnish, she nodded and went with her.

Three weeks later, Gabriella told me:

> I DO want to go to nursery.

I was also learning about giving Gabby clear messages. I had observed my daughter, Eloise, saying 'Goodnight' to her daughter, Anya. Eloise would always say 'Mummy and Daddy love you very much. We'll see you in the morning'. So I developed a similar technique or ritual when leaving Gabby at nursery: 'Pop and I and Mummy and Daddy and Nicole love you very much. Have a lovely time and we'll see you later.'
One day, Gabby (3y 4m 29d) announced:

> 'Rhea is my best friend!'

A few months later, Nicole was off school poorly and Gabriella (3y 7m 9d) decided she did not want to go to nursery. After a bit of persuasion, we:

> got to nursery just before Rhea and, once she saw Rhea, Gabby was very happy to go off with her to get nail varnish on.

During this year, being with her best friend became a strong reason to be at nursery. Rhea lived in another part of town so their parents arranged 'playdates' for the two girls while at nursery and, subsequently, when they went to different schools. Gabriella also made other friends, including a little Ukranian boy whose parents planned to send him to the same school as Gabby. As a family, we were reassured that there would be at least one familiar face for Gabby at school. As it turned out, the boy's family returned to the Ukraine during the summer holidays so he did not turn up at school. However, as you will see, Gabby very soon made some firm friends at school as she had done at nursery.

Links with Theory

Social relationships are widely recognized as being important for young children's identity, well-being and future academic success

(Vygotsky 1986, 1978; Dunn 1993; Oh and Lee 2019). Vygotsky viewed relationships and the social context as one of the main sources of development and learning. Vygotsky believed that what first appears on the social plane is internalized and becomes part of a child's thinking (Vygotsky 1978). I believe that Gabriella was learning from her friends all the time. The opportunity to interact with her cousin, Anya, also provided Gabby with a slightly different relationship to learn from. Months later, Gabby made many comparisons between herself and Anya.

Dunn (1993) found that 'shared humour', among other dimensions, is an important aspect of friendships and I am sure that this was the case for Gabby and Rhea, judging by the giggles that accompanied any mention of 'poo'. Oh and Lee found that 'shared meanings' and 'respect for their play' were important to the two Korean children they interviewed in the United States about 'Who is a friend?' (2019: 659). I think it is interesting that the focus on friends has arisen at the same time as a strong urge to create role play, which requires shared understandings and motivation.

Role Play

The role play that Gabriella engaged in could be described as 'socio-dramatic' play, as she clearly drew on her first-hand experiences and re-enacted many scenarios in which she had been involved (Faulkner 1995). During this year, Gabby spent almost all her time with us in role, often involving Pop and me. It would be impossible to communicate the extent and frequency of these scenarios so I have selected three observations of frequently repeated episodes of play:

1. Gabby (3y 27d) and I came home about 11am and she has continued with pretend game with baby and teddy – going to sleep covered up on the floor, waking up, talking to self constantly – going home, putting car in garage, taking baby on bus. Said to me: 'It's baby's birthday'. I said: 'What happens?' Gabby: 'She gets presents . . . and her friends come', gesturing 'my teddy and your teddy'. Me: 'Who's doing the food?' Gabby: 'Me – a cake.' Me: 'What number is on the cake? How many candles?' Gabby: 'Baby is one – one candle. I'm three – I had three candles on my cake.' When baby fell down, she picked her up and gestured as though putting a dummy in her mouth . . . While on bus: 'Oh! I need my seatbelt on. Sorry, driver!'' (This was repeated almost daily with

variations, such as going to work and taking 'baby' to nursery and 'big brother' to school once Gabby started school).

2. Gabby (3y 7m 21d) played dentists for a long time, sparked off by looking at Pop's (reclining) chair, which she said was like a dentist's chair. Firstly, I was the dentist examining baby's, Gabriella's and teddy's teeth. (She directed me). I said baby's and Gabby's were fine but teddy must have been eating too many sweets and biscuits and not cleaning his teeth. After a while, we reversed roles and Gabby became the dentist and I had to go for an appointment with baby and teddy. Over time, Pop was promoted to being the reception-ist and Gabby would 'read' magazines in the waiting room and pay by card.

3. Gabby (3y 11m) wanted to play that teddy was my little boy and I was taking him to nursery and she was the teacher. She told the children a story 'Hairy Toe', which she had borrowed from Shelley. She adopted 'teacherese' when talking to the children (high pitched like 'motherese'). She took him to the beach area (at nursery) and forest school (miming putting on waterproofs and going on the minibus). She made two home visits and even explained to him that she was going on holi-day 'for two weeks' and that he needed to choose another family worker to be with while she was away: 'It could be Diane or Hayley'. I asked where she was going and she said 'To a hotel'.

In all these scenarios, Gabriella clearly drew accurately on her first-hand experiences.

Links with Theory

Katherine Nelson (1986) talked about 'social scripts' that children acquire from taking part in social situations. These become increasingly complex. More recently, the term 'social schemas' has been coined to describe 'co-created narratives' that become cultural rituals, such as what happens on birthdays (Delafield-Butt 2018: 72).

Another aspect that I think is important is the 'affordance' of the environment; that is, what an environment, including people, 'affords' children in terms of opportunities for play or interaction (Gibson 1986). The 'dentist's' scenario above was sparked by the similarity of a reclining chair to the chair at the dentist. On other occasions, a trip to the 'doctor's' was prompted by spotting a long

Pic 4.2 'Gabby in Role'

shoehorn in our hall, referred to as a 'walking stick'. At 3y 8m 8d, Gabriella asked me for a bag:

> I gave her a small beauty bag, a 'freebie' from one of our flights. She then proceeded to go on holiday to Latvia by plane with baby and Teddy Tom.

Reflections

We sometimes found opportunities to offer ideas to extend Gabby's play, for example language or resources:

> Have you been asking parents about children's play at home or what interests and intrigues them on outings with their family?
> Think about the ways in which you might support children's role play and friendships. Are you able to allow children to take the lead in role play scenarios?

Schemas

During this year, Gabriella continued exploring a cluster of schemas. However, 'enveloping', 'enclosing' and 'seriating' very much came to the fore.

Enveloping

I noticed that some of Gabriella's language related to the schemas she was exploring. For example:

> Gabby (3y 8d) played throwing dice and golf practice balls. Talked about them 'disappearing' when she couldn't see where they had landed (I had not heard her use that word before – things 'disappear' when they are 'enveloped').

Gabriella frequently 'enveloped' objects with cloth or tissues and covered her hands with paint whenever she painted. We talked about removing small objects prior to Anya's visit. Gabby (3y 26d) got into 'hiding' things from Anya:

> Gabby threw a dice and two magnetic ladybirds behind our big couch. Then she shut 'her' bedroom door 'so Anya doesn't go in there' (she had only slept there one night!).

(She was 'enveloping' or hiding objects that Anya might put in her mouth but also decided the spare room was 'out of bounds' to her cousin.) Another reference to being enveloped followed:

> We were in the soft room. Gabby (3y 27d) talked about 'sinking' into the balls.

Again this use of language seemed connected with being 'enveloped'.

At nursery, Gabby buried her feet in the sand to make them 'disappear'. At home, she would ask me to close the curtains, 'enveloping' the light so that she could play that it was night-time. One day, we went to the library:

> I happened to pick out a book entitled *The Dark*, about a little boy called Lazlo who was afraid of the dark. I read it to Gabby (3y 2m 27d) at least 10 times at her request and then she sat at the table and pretended to read it.

We saw in the last section that having her nails 'enveloped' in varnish settled Gabby at nursery. Gabby often played at the bathroom sink, making bubbles, 'enveloping' her chin with bubbles, 'like Santa', or her nails with soap, 'like nail varnish'.

Enclosing

'Enclosing' and 'enveloping' seem to be closely linked. So it is not surprising that Gabriella also became interested in 'enclosing' at this time, both in her actions and representations. Gabby frequently played with Teddy Tim's scarf and, when she was 3y 5m 2d, I noted she:

> managed to put Teddy Tim's scarf across as a seat belt on the buggy – was pleased with herself.

This was a sort of 'enclosure' to stop baby from falling out of the buggy. A few weeks later, I noted:

> Gabby (3y 6m 10d) can draw an 'enclosure' with 'enclosures' inside – she drew her first face a couple of weeks ago. Today, she drew an 'enclosure' with 'enclosures' inside and added her 'name' and 'baby's name' (curved shapes).

Pic 4.3 'A spider' – an enclosure with enclosures inside

Pic 4.4 Pretend writing and thinking about attachment

18.5.16
Gabby was 'writing' and
saying what she was
writing
"You can look at This
if you feel sad and you
know I'm coming
back for you"
She drew her frog
(rubber ring frog was
on floor)

Seriating

A few months after Anya's visit, Gabriella suddenly started using a lot of comparative language, demonstrating her understanding of 'seriating':

> Gabby (3y 7m 22d) frequently compares herself with Anya, pointing out she's 'bigger' than Anya and Anya is 'smaller' than her.

Also at 3y 8m 8d, during one of her many pretend games with animal figures:

> Big Bear says to Baby Bear: 'You're smaller than me'.

> Said there was a competition to see who had the 'loudest' voice. Then pretended to be Teddy shouting loudly and said 'he winned'.

'Louder' is the comparative term, 'loudest' is the superlative term and 'winned' is a 'virtuous error' – when we follow a grammatical rule without knowing the exception (won).

Links with Theory

According to Athey (2007: 42), 'the relationship between action and the effects of action is a central concept of constructivism', so the idea that Gabby recognized that objects were 'disappearing' indicates that she knew what was happening as a result of her action – when she 'enveloped' something, it 'disappeared'. 'Sinking' seems a bit more removed and almost metaphorical, as we often talk about a boat sinking rather than a person. Gabriella loved water play and Evita reported that Gabriella spends long periods of time in the bath 'experimenting' with toys so she probably learned about 'sinking' in water and then applied it to herself in the ball pool. In using this language, Gabby was possibly focusing on the process or procedure that would result in her body being 'enveloped' by the balls (Athey 2007: 48).

Gabby's interest in 'enclosing' enabled her to symbolically represent writing and faces at this time, which was a development in skill and knowledge.

Although Gabriella had played with lots of objects that were seriated (for example, seriated beakers, Russian dolls), this language only appeared some time later when she seemed to fully understand language like 'bigger than'. She did not only apply this in a size context but also in relation to sound ('loudest') and colour ('lighter' and 'darker').

New Language

Gabriella's language was fluent by the age of three so I only noted down when she used a word I had not heard her use before, as you saw in the schemas section. Gabriella loved stories and was told lots at home, at our home and at the library. One day, she was playing in the garden with Pop and the hose. She had the garage key and accidentally opened the garage door, as the key works remotely and is sensitive to touch:

Gabby (3y 1d) came to me with the garage key saying 'I opened it, sorry!' (First time I'd heard her saying sorry.) She had closed it as well by then.

Part of 'enveloping' was a game where she would hide the dice somewhere in our bungalow and would give us a 'clue' about where to find it. At 3y 4m 24d, she said:

'It's where you sleep.'

Gabby (3y 4m) was also noticing environmental print when she told me that a sign meant 'No lipstick outside'.

At 3y 4m 29d, she began adding 'actually' to her sentences and also talked about 'trying her best'. When she was playing with soap at the sink (3y 7m 18d), she pretended they were fish:

> Gabby put them in and out of the water, saying she was putting them 'on dry land'.

I noted when she used the word 'complicated' for the first time (3y 11m 22d).

Links with Theory

Children are learning language at the same time as it appears in its 'ideal form' in their environment, as Vygotsky pointed out (1986). This could lead us to believe that we learn language mainly through imitation; however, the use of language in the right context is a fairly sophisticated achievement. Gabby's adding of 'actually' to her sentences may be in imitation of what she had heard but most of her other new language, especially the conceptual language such as 'disappearing' and 'sinking', demonstrated conceptual understanding.

Scientific, Technological and Mathematical Development

This was a year when 'Why?' questions came to the fore and when Gabriella experimented and had 'working theories' about processes that she was able to articulate.

Science

Gabby (3y 1m 10d) was playing with bubbles in the garden when she reasoned,

> 'If I leave the wand in the bubbles for longer, I'll get bigger bubbles'.

On the same day,

> Gabby picked up a highlighter pen. She took the lid off and squeezed it before commenting, 'It's not lighting up' (Gabby was seeking a connection between the name of an object and its function).

At nursery in the beach area,

> Gabby (3y 5m 2d) struggled to make a sandcastle using a large bucket, which was heavy and unwieldy. . .much more successful with filling a small cone and tipping it over. She could replicate the cone almost perfectly and then took great pleasure in 'smashing' it with her foot before repeating her actions.

At our home,

> Gabby (3y 7m 18d) played at the sink in our bathroom: firstly dropped each of the three bars of soap in, saying 'Does it float?' Each of them sank. She then dropped in the plastic bottle containing liquid soap and this floated.

At her home,

> We were watching 'Packman'. Gabby (3y 8m 6d) asked 'Why do they fly?' (Ghosts in the story). I explained that it was pretend, not real. We talked about what does fly – birds, planes, helicopters, flies, dragonflies, bees, wasps. This led to talking about paper aeroplanes – Gabby went and got some paper from their computer room (she can reach the light!) for me to make an aeroplane. I explained how I make it 'streamlined'. She practised throwing it – I suggested how she could use her body to throw it upwards so it travelled in an arc and went further. She did this a few times.

Gabby (3y 11m) reflected on the life cycle,

> We were driving past Pen Green, when Gabby said 'I used to go to the Baby Nest'. Me 'Did you enjoy it?' Gabby 'No, I like the Den – I go to the big nursery now – then I'll go to school. . .and then work. . .and then I'll die'. She added 'When I'm very old'. Me 'Yes I hope it'll be a very long time before you die'. (Death was a strong interest of Gabby's at this time. You will see other references to age and death in the section on Maths).

Technology

Gabriella received an iPad for her third birthday. She used this more at home than when she was with us but I noted:

> Gabby (3y 4m) has learned the password for her iPad (not taught but by 'intent participation'). She wanted to show me several

times that *she* can make it work. She also sang the ABC song featured on YouTube and then repeated it without YouTube. She is really pleased with herself.

Mathematics

Counting

Her interests ranged from counting to games to time and age. With regard to *counting*, I had set a timer for her nail varnish to dry:

> Gabby (3y 8m 8d) counted down: '1,2,3,4,5,6,7,8,9,10,0' (so we can deduce that Gabby could recite the counting numbers in order but does not yet realize that, for a countdown, you recite them backwards. However, she does know that a countdown ends with 0).

It was more than 3 months later when I noted:

> Gabby (3y 11m 30d) can almost count backwards from 10 to 0, struggled with 8.

> Can almost count to 20 but missed out 15 twice.

Games

With regard to *games*, I noted when Gabby was 3y 4m 28d:

> We played Snap – she loved winning and kept telling me I was the loser'.

> We played cards and Gabby (3y 10m 30d) recognized all of the numbers. She got a bit confused between 6 and 9 but when I suggested looking at the top number on the card, she got it right just about every time (number at bottom is upside down so 9 resembles 6 and vice versa).

Playing cards also helped with her letter recognition:

> Gabby didn't know at first what the ace was called so I pointed to the A and said 'A for Anya and A for Asda and this A means ace' (I had made her an alphabet book for her third birthday and these were examples with which she was familiar). I also differentiated between king, queen and jack and she got that right away and named them correctly each time.

Pic 4.5 Alphabet book

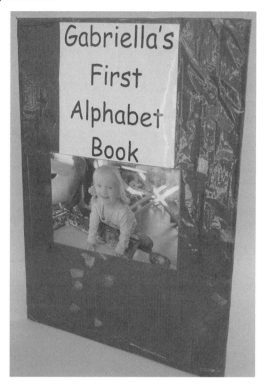

Then there was the issue of winning and losing so, when she had got the hang of the game:

> I won the odd game. She was upset at first but I explained: 'It's a game and you have to learn to lose as well as win'. Gabby seemed to understand, although she continued to enjoy winning.

Later that day, Evita sent me a video of Gabby teaching her to play cards so I could see she had understood and remembered.

Time and Age

Gabriella (3y 7m) asked me how old I was. I responded with '69'. Gabby (3y 7m 22d) continued this conversation:

> Gabby: 'Are you a little bit old?'
> Me: 'Yes.'

Gabby: 'When you are very old, you will die?'

Me: 'Yes.'

Gabby: 'And when Pop is very old, he will die?'

Me: 'Yes.'

Gabby: 'I'll miss you.'

Gabby moved on from thinking about the whole life cycle to thinking about time more specifically:

Gabby (3y 8d) was playing with two babies. Put them to bed and said they would sleep for 'an hour'.

When Gabriella was 3y 9m 26d, I noted that:

Lots of 'yesterday, I . . .' and went on to talk about Nicole: 'She used to come to the soft room when she was seven – 8-year-olds aren't allowed' and 'I gonna be seven'. Also talked about the 'next episode' of a programme on TV.

The following day,

Gabby and Nicole use an egg timer to time cleaning their teeth. Today, Gabby borrowed it and said she was going to see how long it took to get to my house.

She asked: 'How long to your house?'

Me: 'About five to ten minutes.'

Gabby: 'Are we nearly there?'

Me: 'About halfway.'

Later that day, Gabby incorporated time into her role play:

'I going to set the clock (the egg timer) how much time to pick Rhea up,' and then 'Time to pick Rhea up'.

When I complained that the bedroom was a bit chilly, Gabby said 'I 18 so I can stay here by myself'. (I'm now in role and living at Rhea's house).

Gabby: 'If you like, I can visit you sometimes.'

Me: 'Will you visit me tomorrow?'

Gabby 'Yes, when it morning.'

I could tell that Gabby (3y 10m 11d) was thinking about time when:

> I said: 'We need to go for Mummy in two minutes.'
>
> Gabby: 'Is two minutes a long time?'
>
> Me: 'No – it'll go very quickly'.
>
> Gabby: 'Is it a long time when you clean your teeth for two minutes?'
>
> Me: 'It does seem a long time.'
>
> Gabriella seemed to realize that it was relative to what she was doing.

Links with Theory

With regard to science, Gabriella was vocalizing a 'working theory' about what she was thinking would happen, as well as experimenting with a variety of materials to see what would happen. Children's 'working theories' have been given a lot of attention in the New Zealand context and examples show that we frequently 'underestimate children's competence' (Peters and Davis 2015: 260). Listening to children's ideas is highly recommended, both in terms of their motivation and feeling valued.

Gabriella was picking up some wide-ranging ideas about mathematics at this time. The examples show that the recitation of numbers in order was coming on and that she developed an interest in 'duration', as her cousin Georgia had at around the same age (Arnold 1999). Gabby was also sorting out in her mind rules about when she could or could not do things, such as play in the soft room when you are seven but not eight, and stay by yourself when you are 18.

Anomalies

Around this time Gabriella seemed to be establishing the 'order' of things. We usually discovered what she was thinking through conversations or questions:

> Gabby (3y 6m 24d) noticed a wooden puzzle on Pop's side table. I said: 'Pop got it for Christmas but hasn't been able to solve it yet.' She sat on Pop's chair, leaned back and said '*You* buy us toys' (meaning that adults buy children toys, not the other way around).

A similar thing happened later that day:

> Pop said he liked a car Gabby had got for Christmas.
>
> Gabby: 'But it's *pink*!'
>
> Pop: 'But it's a *car*!' (Here, gender stereotypes were being challenged by Pop liking a pink car).

More questions about gender followed:

> Gabby (3y 7m 11d) asked: 'Is Anya a girl?', which led to conversations about length of hair and gender. She accepted that girls can have long or short hair but was less convinced that boys and men can have long hair. I told her that her daddy had long hair when he was little because he didn't like getting his hair cut. Also that when her daddy was grown up and went to India, his hair grew long and he had it in a ponytail. She didn't believe this and said: 'Men don't have ponytails'.

Links with Theory

You may see the term 'schema' (plural schemata) used in traditional psychology to describe the store of knowledge that children build up about particular aspects of their experience. Here, Gabriella was in the process of building knowledge about gender. Inevitably, her experience of the world was limited at this stage and she questioned things that did not seem to fit in with her current ideas.

With regard to gender specifically, there has been a great deal of research into how children develop their ideas about gender over the years (Cvencek and Meltzoff 2015). Boys' underachievement and the lack of women in professions that require maths or science degrees are commonly discussed. It is felt that stereotypes should be challenged during the early years, particularly as women currently dominate early years education in the Western world, despite some European countries making great efforts to recruit male early childhood practitioners (Spence and Clapton 2018).

Reflections

Children's questions are a fount of information about their interests.

Recall and discuss any questions children have asked you today. Record questions children ask over the space of the next week. What do these tell you about what you could plan for the children?

SUMMARY

In this chapter, we saw Gabriella grow up from 3 to 4 years old. What seemed most important to her during this year were:

- friendships – her 'best friend' became a firm friend
- role play – much of Gabby's time with us was spent in 'role'
- schemas – enveloping, enclosing and seriating came to the fore.

I also noted:

- New language, some of which was connected to the schemas she was exploring.
- Science, technology and mathematical development, including some of Gabby's 'working theories'.
- Anomalies Gabby noticed, particularly in relation to her current conceptualization of gender.

As far as the pedagogy is concerned:

Intent	Implementation	Impact
We wanted to help Gabby get over the loss of her precious teddy	Giving her a new teddy for her birthday identical to the one she had lost	Gabby accepts the new teddy. They become inseparable
Settling her into a new nursery space	Talking to her family worker, Shelley, about her interest in 'enveloping'. Shelley provided nail varnish	She wants to go to nursery to further explore 'enveloping'. She feels understood
Adopting a ritual at drop-off time	Using the same phrase to signal leaving her at nursery	She is more certain that she will manage without me there
Supporting her knowledge and thinking	Letting her take the lead but participate in her role play	Increased understanding of social situations

Intent	Implementation	Impact
Helping her increase her conceptual understanding	Using language and resources to support her dominant schemas	She uses language appropriately to demonstrate conceptual understanding
Feeding her curiosity	Having conversations to support her puzzles and resources to explore, e.g. paper planes	Gains some scientific knowledge
Helping her with recognition of number symbols	Playing games	She can match and name numbers
Continuing to feed her curiosity	Responding honestly to her questions about dying	She gets a sense of the human life cycle

5   From 4 to 5 Years

Gabriella's world continued to expand during this year. She started attending school at 4y 2m 25d, a 'summer-born' child. Some children starting school were more than 9 months older than Gabby, as the cut-off date for starting school in England is currently being 4 years old by the end of August. During the Reception year, schools in England adhere to the Early Years Foundation Stage Statutory Framework, which is intended to be play based, although the trend from 2017 has been to introduce a slightly more formal curriculum-style approach, including daily phonics and mathematics.

In terms of Gabriella's home life, she and her family visited family in Latvia for two weeks that summer and we joined them for a long weekend in the middle. I had a special birthday in October, so Gabby and family joined us in Tenerife for the half-term week. In December, Pop and I made our final trip to Australia and spent seven weeks there. Our daughter and family who lived there returned to England just before we returned.

During this year, I often looked after Gabriella and her sister before and after school but not for such long periods of time as previously. However, we often spent time with the family going out for meals or eating at our home or theirs.

Interestingly, what came to the fore when I studied the data for this year fits well with the areas of the curriculum as described in the Foundation Stage Statutory Framework (DfE 2017):

- Physical development
- Personal, social and emotional development
- Communication and language
- Mathematics, including games with rules
- Understanding the world

The first three are considered 'prime areas' and the second two are referred to as 'specific areas'. I have included any 'literacy' in 'Communication and Language' and 'expressive arts and design' did not seem to figure prominently in the data. These are the two other specific areas in the document (DfE 2017).

Physical Development

Much of Gabby's physical development continued in local parks or going out on her balance bike but one day:

> Gabby (4y 25d) made an 'obstacle course' in our living room by lining up objects across the room and walking on them. (This became a frequently practised game).

Gabriella's Opi (Grandad) lives in Latvia in the countryside, 200 metres from the sea, so the fortnight spent in Latvia was mostly out of doors. When we visited, I noted:

> Gabby (4y 1m 11d) loves the beach and sea, building sandcastles and having her feet buried. She was playing frisbee outside with Paul and me. She did not realize she needed to bring the frisbee across her body from left to right so we showed her the technique.
>
> Gabby loved climbing up a mound in the garden and sliding down. Gabby and Nicole played hide and seek several times.

On our last day, we went to the open-air museum where Opi works:

> Gabby loved sitting on a large stone frog and balancing on a wall.

Back at home, we went to East Carlton Park:

> Gabby (4y 2m 1d) liked the swings, accessible roundabout and (challenging) slide. The first rung of the ladder to climb up to the slide was level with Gabby's waist, so climbing up was challenging each time. The slide was high and covered over. Gabby told me that the first time she closed her eyes but subsequently went on lots of times without closing her eyes. She didn't want to leave and negotiated five extra turns.

Gabriella was pleased that she was now old enough to attend a playscheme with Nicole so they both attended for four days during August, when there were trips out and lots of outdoor activities. Gabby (at 4y 2m 15d) recalled that, over a year earlier, she and her friend had been playing tag when Nicole came to the same area with playscheme.

Gabriella started school at 4y 2m 25d. The school she attends has a lovely covered and outdoor area attached to the Reception classes so much of her time was spent out of doors on the climbing equipment. However, she clearly was not sure what PE was because at first she looked forward to it, then got a bit worried and finally (at 4y 3m 16d), she:

> told us she enjoyed PE and explained how they had to go to another room and find a space and stand on one leg. (I am sure there was more to PE than this, but this was what Gabby recalled).

Meanwhile, at our home:

> Gabby (4y 3m 10d) came to us after school and wanted to do lots of things she's done before . . . Jumping on the bed, being a teddy bear, monkey, lizard, rainbow etc. Then she moved all the cushions in the living room to make a soft room on the floor. Then cutting out, making 'squares' and 'triangles'. Also drew and did 'G' several times.

During the October half-term in Tenerife, I noted:

> Gabby (4y 4m 25d) loved the pools and the zipline (once she was brave enough to go on).

Pic 5.1 Jumping on the bed

At this time, Gabby was wearing armbands in the pool and starting to jump into the shallow water. Her name was down at our local pool for the very popular swimming lessons, which she subsequently attended.

Shortly after we returned from Australia:

> Gabriella (4y 9m 20d) learned to ride her two-wheeler bike without stabilizers. She was very proud of this achievement.

As well as Gabby's large movements and balance and co-ordination developing, she was also becoming more proficient with small movements:

> Gabby (4y 10m 9d) was playing on the computer, typing like a typist but also typing her name and 'baby' and 'Are you OK?' Asked me: 'How do you spell OR?' I could not understand until she said the full sentence: 'Are you OK?'

A few days later, I picked her up from school:

> Gabby wanted to stay and play in the playground. One boy had his scooter and she was organizing two boys and herself to take turns.

The same day, Gabby played 'piggy in the middle' with Pop and me and also lifted up our wooden stools to prove how strong she was becoming.

Gabby (4y 10m 21d) came to our house for a couple of hours after school. She brought her scooter and was keen to show us her new tricks:

> Gabby jumped onto the moving scooter, stood sideways on it and rode with one foot on the scooter and one in the air. Also rode really fast on our driveway, almost crashing into the garage door.

Links with Theory

Apart from PE as part of the school curriculum, the challenges were set by Gabby and resulted in deep involvement, demonstrated by her wanting to continue, for example, at the park and in the playground after school (Laevers 1997). Deep involvement results in 'deep-level learning' according to Laevers (1997), who draws on Csikszentmihalyi's research on 'flow', the feeling of time standing still and deep concentration that engages us fully when optimally challenged (1992).

Gabby was either at her home, our home or on holiday when these observations were made and, naturally, chose how to engage with what each environment afforded (Gibson 1986). In order to achieve this kind of deep involvement, Ephgrave (2018: 140) recommends 'child-initiated play for the maximum amount of time possible' in settings. So, in Reception classes, I believe that most learning occurs when most of the activity is child initiated.

> **Reflections**
> What sorts of opportunities are on offer in your setting for physical play?
> Do you record levels of involvement by individual children?
> How can you ensure a good balance between adult-led and child-led activity in your setting?

Personal, Social and Emotional Development

Looking back over this first year at school for Gabriella, what stands out are new friendships, challenges and confidence gained. That summer prior to starting school, going to visit her mother's family in Latvia was very exciting, but when *we* arrived Gabby (4y 1m 11d) seemed:

> quite confused to have Evita, Paul, Opi, Pop and me all at once so there was lots of crying, screaming and refusing to do what we wanted her to do.

It all seemed too much and I think what we saw was a kind of transition from being with us individually at home to being in a totally different context with all of us (possibly) making demands on her. However, Gabby settled down and, on our last full day in Latvia, we went to Jūrmala, a nearby town. After having a snack in a café, I took Gabby to the toilet. She was in there for ages and, after a while, said:

> 'Imagine . . . if you were wearing shorts and no knickers?' She then went through each member of the family, posing the same question and laughing very loudly afterwards. (These were the sort of jokes Gabby and her friend shared).

On another occasion that summer, I was looking after Gabby (4y 2m 11d) and Nicole at their home. We were getting ready to go out. I walked into the living room and saw her leaning into a plastic bag. I panicked and said 'Don't do that, Gabby!'. It was rare for me to ask her not to do something:

> Gabby got very angry and ran upstairs (to her bedroom I thought) but when I followed a couple of minutes later, she'd gone right up to the third floor and woken Paul (who was sleeping after a 12-hour nightshift). She would not have anything to do with me so I left her with Paul. About five minutes later, she came downstairs and we went out. In the car, we talked about what had happened and I reassured her that I wasn't telling her off but was just concerned because I love her.

Gabby's First Day at School

I do not think we always realize the pressure children feel when we talk about big changes like starting school. Gabriella was 4y 2m 25d when she started school and the school policy was to start all children full time from day one. Gabby's mother is very good at celebrating special occasions like this, so Evita reported:

> Gabby was quite grumpy and tired when she got up but then opened her special present (a Minion alarm clock) and cheered up. She went into school OK and seemed OK when Evita and Paul went to pick her up. She told them what she had been doing but clearly was not sure of the routine, as she did not get up right away when the teacher said she could go. We met the family for a meal at a local restaurant after school that day as a celebration. Gabby brought her alarm clock and showed us the features. We went back to their home for coffee and cake. Gabby and Nicole were playing and got the computer chair out. Gabby sat on the chair and said she was 'the queen' and her 'guard' (Nicole) pushed her around.

A couple of weeks later, they:

> came to our house after school. Gabby (4y 3m 10d) looked a head taller – hair in a ponytail. I asked her permission for photos of her to go into the Pen Green 0–3s book. She was enthusiastic: 'Yes – that's my favourite fish! That's my favourite rocking horse … !' She wanted to do lots of things she's done before.

Just after half-term and our holiday together in Tenerife, I took Gabriella (4y 4m 27d) to school one morning:

> As we got near the classroom and Gabby saw her teacher, she did a little dance (of pleasure?) and connected with her teacher.

Another Change

We had prepared Gabriella and Nicole for the fact that we were going to Australia for Christmas and would be away for seven weeks. However, the day before we were leaving:

> This morning, we played Snap and Gabby (4y 6m 5d) had a major 'paddy' when I shouted 'Snap!' before her. She went upstairs, screamed, cried and stamped her feet . . . I left her for a while and she calmed down when I told her Anya and Aunty Eloise were on FaceTime from Australia.

We kept in contact while we were away, and Gabby seemed much more grown up and confident on our return. She talked to me about some of her friends at school:

> Gabby (4y 10m 1d) said: 'I don't think I'll be Amy or David's friend when I go back to school. I have to keep protecting David. If he falls over, he cries and I have to drag him to the teacher. If I fall over, I cry and I just go and tell the teacher'.

Gabby was obviously recognizing her own strength and confidence. She articulated this to me:

> Georgia (her cousin, aged 26y) arrived. Gabby (4y 10m 21d) was really chatty, telling Georgia she goes to school and she's going to be five 'in 2 months', also writing her name and two sentences to show Georgia how she can write . . . On the way home, Gabby said to me, 'When I was two, I was shy of Georgia but now I'm not shy'. (Brilliant the confidence she has gained since she's been at school.)

A few weeks after this, I was at their house one morning, when:

> Gabby said 'Come and see Mummy's bedroom!' She showed me her table and chairs on the landing, soft toys at the top of the stairs (third floor) and Gabby's bedside table in 'Mummy's bedroom'. Then she showed me her dad's bedside table in her room. She seemed quite excited and pleased. I did not enquire further. (See below for an explanation).

Links with Theory

Looking back, this seemed to be a year of ups and downs for Gabriella. Going to Latvia and starting school were both exciting prospects, but, when viewed from a young child's perspective, they evoked feelings of fear and anxiety as well as pleasure. For the last 25 years, I have considered emotional well-being through the lens of the Leuven Well-being Signals and Scale (Laevers 1997). The signals and scale enable us, as adults, to think about how a child presents and what might be going on in terms of feelings. So when Gabby rushed upstairs to wake her dad up when she felt I had 'told her off', I realized that she felt hurt and embarrassed and was reacting to or externalizing those feelings, although she herself could probably not articulate them at that time. This was when it was helpful for her father and I to contain those feelings and give them back to her in a manageable form (through words) (Bion 1962). Luckily, we were able to talk through what had happened in the car afterwards.

Another emotional outburst occurred just before we were going to Australia when I beat Gabby at Snap. In this instance, I noted that Gabby seemed to almost need an excuse to be angry with me. Possibly, she felt angry that we were going away to spend time with her cousins and would miss us.

On the other hand, there were several occasions when Gabby showed us that her well-being was extremely high, for example when she was settled at school, when doing a little dance of 'chuffedness' when she saw her teacher, by gaining confidence, when she articulated how she was caring for other children, and when she was chatting to Georgia and no longer shy with her (Tait 2005).

With regard to the final observation, her parents had shared with us that they were thinking of separating. I was not sure of what Gabby and her sister understood of this decision, so I did not comment but just listened.

Reflections

How do you monitor children's emotional well-being?

Are you aware of 'containing' the anxieties of the children in your care?

Have you thought about sharing your ideas about emotional well-being with parents and carers so that you have the language to discuss children's emotional well-being on a regular basis?

Communication and Language

During this year, Gabriella continued to role play when she was with us, as well as articulating her ideas more clearly, using some metaphorical language and beginning to read. The first use of metaphorical language:

> Gabby (4y 5d) was playing hiding the dice with Pop. She has now got the hang of being 'warmer' or 'colder' in relation to how close she is to the hidden dice.

The same day, Gabby repeated her 'dentists' game,

> Gabby adopted an authoritative tone. A new variation was that she went for a run in her lunch break and came back a little breathless.

I noted:

> Gabby (4y 10d) has taken to using Anya's car seat, which is in the spare room, to take her 'babies' to nursery, to go to Asda etc. The seatbelt is very tricky to fasten. Today, she mastered it and kept strapping in her two babies and they kept 'jumping out' so she had to undo and do up the tricky fastener.

Pic 5.2 Creating enclosures and trajectories and bringing in humour

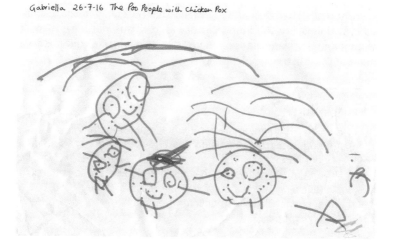

Gabriella 26-7-16 The Poo People with Chicken Pox

Pic 5.3 Early writing

I noted Gabby doing some recognizable marks:

> Gabby (4y 25d) (accidentally) did a 'G', an 'N' and an 'M'. She was very aware of how to write 'M', saying 'Up, down, up, down'. She also wrote 1, 2, 3', made other marks for '4, 5, 6, 7, 8, 9 and then wrote '10'.

Pic 5.4 An attempt to write 'Gabriella', plus pretend writing and drawing

Two days later. I noted some new language:

> Gabby was on her bike in the garden and said 'I'm taking a shortcut'.

While we were in Latvia, we went on a 'barefoot walk' that involved walking on different surfaces and terrains. Gabby was 4y 1m 13d and I noticed her language:

> Daddy's 'leading' and we're 'catching up' with Daddy.

Gabby was also noticing some of the Latvian language and commented she could remember the word for 'flag' ('karogs') as it is like 'carrots'. Opi said Gabby was understanding quite a lot of Latvian.

Sometimes, Gabby found her own way of explaining something, for example at 4y 2m, when she said to her dad about her iPad:

> 'It was nearly dead at the last week.' (He realized she meant it needed charging.)

Gabriella watched quite lengthy films on TV around this time and loved stories and songs:

> Gabby (4y 3m 14d) was using her CD player and found her *Little Rabbit Foo Foo* CD and book. She listened and sang it word for word and then went through the book repeating it word for word.

During the October half-term in Tenerife, naturally we had all our meals together sitting around a large table:

> Gabby (4y 4m 25d) liked listening to stories about my three younger siblings. She asked me to repeat them again and again at dinner. She wanted to hear stories of them being 'naughty' and also the *My Naughty Little Sister* story about the naughty little sister biting Santa's hand. On the last day as we all had lunch, Gabby made up her own stories (very much based on what I had been telling her, but with little variations) and she would say 'This is a real story' or 'this isn't a real story' before telling it (she was amazing!).

After the half-term, Gabby's school started inviting parents and carers in one morning a week to tell stories to children. At the first one, I told Gabby 'Tell it to the Toucan', in which the word 'jamboree' came up. Gabby wanted to know 'What is a jamboree?' I said, 'A party, I think'. We asked Gabby's teacher, who said, 'A celebration'.

Gabby (at 4y 6m 5d) noticed that one word can have two meanings, for example 'Pop' is her granddad and you can 'pop' a balloon. On the same day, Gabby read the whole of *Miss! Miss!* to Anya and Eloise on FaceTime – I think it was her reading book from school.

Five months later:

> Gabby (4y 11m 19d) took home a plastic sleeve containing three tennis balls and developed a game whereby one of us rolled the tennis balls along the floor and the other 'caught' them in the sleeve . . . She commented that a ball 'escaped' from the sleeve when it fell out.

The following day, we were playing the same game when their cat, Robin, went under a nearby table and appeared to be watching us. Gabby said: 'Robin is our 'audience!'

Links with Theory

The current Early Years Foundation Stage Framework (used for guidance only) divides the topic of 'Communication and Language' into three areas: listening and attention, understanding and speaking (DfE 2017). We can see from the above observations that Gabriella could listen to and tell stories and that she had a sound understanding of what was being said, as well as enquiring about words she had not come across before, such as 'jamboree'. As far as literacy was concerned, she was beginning to take an interest in writing and reading.

Pic 5.5 Writing and drawing becomes more refined for Pop's birthday (4y 9m 1d)

What interested me more was her use of 'escape' when she was referring to the tennis ball falling out of the sleeve. I believe this is personification, a literary device sometimes used in the literature or speech but it is quite sophisticated for a 4-year-old. The other use of language that surprised me was her use of the word 'audience' when referring to her cat seemingly watching us play. This suggests to me some flexibility in thinking, in that Gabby could think about her cat as an 'audience' watching what we were playing. Athey (1990: 134) refers to 'projective space' whereby children can think about objects and people from different points of view.

Mathematics, including Games with Rules

One of Gabby's favourite activities during this year was playing games. These could be games she or we invented like 'catching tennis balls in a plastic sleeve' as described in the last section, or they could be board games or card games. I know from my own children and my older grandchildren that children can learn a lot of maths through playing games (Arnold 1999, 2003). At the beginning of this fifth year in Gabriella's life, I firstly noticed her 'writing numbers 1, 2 and 3' at 4y 4d and then expressing ideas about amounts:

> Pop asked me whether he should put salt and pepper on my lunch. I responded, 'Salt please, just a little bit'. Gabby (4y 18d) explained (gesticulating with her fingers) 'A little bit, like a tiny drop of water'.

Earlier that morning, she had gone to nursery on her balance bike and I said, 'If you fall off, I don't want you to cry for 20 minutes like you did the other day'. Gabby gesticulated with her fingers: 'Just cry a little bit'.

While we were in Latvia, Gabby (4y 1m 11d) and her sister were playing hide and seek:

> The first time they played, Nicole said, 'Count to 20'. Gabby replied, 'I can only count to 10' so I suggested, 'Count to 10 twice' and she did this each time. Not sure how, but by the end of their holiday Gabby could count up to 37 correctly.

Gabby (4y 5m 9d) was talking about Julia, a child in her class:

> I said, 'I don't know her – you'll have to show me'. Gabby thought for a couple of moments and then said 'She comes into school *pretty* early'.

On our return from Australia:

> Gabby (4y 10m) announced, 'My slippers don't fit any more'. She was puzzled and explained, 'My new school shoes are size 8 and my slippers are size 8 but my slippers don't fit. Maybe my feet grow?'

On the same day, Gabby counted up to 110.

A conversation later that day was about Julia. I asked if she had been to Julia's party and whether David (a boy she was friendly with) had also gone. Her reply:

> 'No – he was invited but he had to go somewhere else that day . . . hopefully he can come to mine. I'd like Rhea to see him.'

A few days later:

> We played Snakes and Ladders for a long time. Gabby (4y 10m 9d) focused very much on 'the rules'. She said 'If you throw a six, you get another turn'. Then, halfway through, suddenly said, 'My Mummy said if you throw a one, you get another turn'. I doubted it but Gabby was very convincing, 'My Mummy said', even claiming it was a Latvian rule. So we started again, implementing the new rule. Gabby focused on throwing the dice a long way (not sure if she thought 'big throw equals big number'). We played Snap again for a long time. Gabby dealt the cards this time.

Paul and the two girls came for dinner:

> After dinner, Gabby (4y 11m 18d) brought the 'Pick-n-sticks' to the table and was distributing them and wanting to play some sort of game. Pop suggested each person has a throw of the dice and be given an equivalent number of sticks. When the sticks had run out, we each counted how many we had. Gabby counted hers correctly in a one-to-one correspondence – 14. We played several games.

We continued to play the same games over and over again:

> Played Snap – Gabby (4y 11m 20d) can now deal, is fast at shouting 'SNAP!' but is also able to lose as well as win, although she still *loves* winning.

Links with Theory

Vygotsky argues that imaginary play also has rules; that is, when Gabby was playing 'mother' or 'teacher', she had certain 'rules' implicitly in mind (1978). Similarly, he argues that games with rules create imaginary situations. I find this idea easier to apply to some games than others. For example, Snakes and Ladders creates a 'journey' for each counter, which is bound by rules about what you can and cannot do and the first to reach the 'destination' is the winner. In the process of playing Snakes and Ladders, children learn about the order of numbers up to 100, one-to-one correspondence (moving one square for each dot on the dice), equivalence (number of dots equals number of moves) and direction.

With regard to the Early Years Statutory Framework, Gabby was learning about counting in order, eventually knowing which was 'one more' or 'one less' of a given number (DfE 2017). She was learning to add and subtract using real objects and could share a whole pack of cards between two people.

Gabby's use of the term 'pretty early' indicated that she was 'seriating', or placing Julia's earliness in an order in her thinking; that is, not 'very' early but 'pretty' early (Gruber and Voneche 1977: 383). Her other conversation about hoping David could come to her party as she 'would like Rhea to see him' is another indication that she can think about the world from another person's perspective, which, in mathematical terms, involves a shift from 'topological space notions' to 'projective space notions' (Athey 1990, 2007). In other words, Gabby could think about a situation that had not yet occurred by having a kind of 'cognitive map' in her mind based on her experiences (Athey 2007: 154).

Understanding the World

This topic, as part of the curriculum, is wide ranging, from 'People' to 'The World' to 'Technology'. Noticing changes is part of understanding the world. At the beginning of this year, while still at nursery, Gabby had shown a strong interest in water play and especially in the deep puddles in the outdoor area. She was playing at the bathroom sink at our home:

> Gabby (4y 4d) played with a large bar of soap (she called it 'shark') and three smaller bars of soap ('dolphins'), then shark became 'Mother Dolphin' whose babies went to her . . . Really liked filling the soap dish with water and displacing the water with the glass dish that fits in the outer dish and/or with the dolphins'. I noted the following day: 'Still *loves* puddles.

In Latvia:

> Gabby (4y 1m 11d) built 'paradise' on a mound of sand out-
> side Opi's with a bucket and spade, and on the day we visited
> the open-air museum, she loved finding blueberries (?) grow-
> ing wild.

Links with Theory

Firstly, we saw Gabriella finding out about 'displacement' through her explorations (science). Again, Vygotsky is helpful in his idea that children develop 'spontaneous concepts' through their explorations but that these need to connect with 'scientific concepts' taught in school (1986). His idea is that these early explorations 'mediate' the learning of scientific concepts (Vygotsky 1986: 161).

A Question About Family

Sometimes, Gabriella would ask a question, seemingly out of the blue with no follow up. For example:

> Gabby (4y 1m 29d): 'What was your dad's name?'

Me: 'Tom.'

Links with Theory

Gabby asked questions over a long period of time, while working out in her head the relationships within our family (history). As far as she could see, most of us were adults so it took many questions for her to really understand the three generations.

An Interest in Maps

At other times, I could see where her interest came from:

> The family are going to London for the weekend. When I arrived
> this morning, Gabby (4y 2m 14d) had the little book about
> London I bought them ages ago – the best thing about the
> book (for Gabby) was that when you open the first or last
> page, the map unfolds. She loved looking at the map and find-
> ing the London Eye. She kept saying it was near the 'lake'

(she meant the River Thames). It was very small writing so Gabby fetched a magnifying glass so we could see it more clearly . . . Only the previous day, when I had said, 'I need to go into work', Gabby had said 'Your work is near my playscheme', then gesticulated with two hands: 'My playscheme is here' and 'Your work is here'.

Links with Theory

Gabby seemed to be becoming interested in maps and where things are located (geography). Athey mentions 'proximity' in terms of 'spatial organization' but Gabby recognized a landmark (the London Eye) represented symbolically on a map and commented on its proximity to the river (2007: 70).

Making More Connections

A few weeks later, Evita reported:

> I heard Gabby (4y 3m 12d) and Nicole talking – Nicole was very upset as she'd realized that her mummy and daddy will die one day. Gabby replied, 'Just think – there'll just be the two of us in the house and we'll be able to do whatever we want!'

Not long after this, Gabriella (4y 3m 18d) got interested in the concept of falling in love:

> Gabby wanted to know why I married Pop. She asked 'Why didn't you marry my Daddy?' I explained that he's my son.

A few days later:

> Gabby wanted me to play upstairs. She was sitting in a chair facing the bed. Big Teddy was on the bed. She said she was pretending to marry Big Teddy and went off to find another teddy for me to marry (but got distracted so the game ended).

Near Bonfire Night (a festival celebrated in the UK), Nicole and I were talking about Guy Fawkes trying to blow up the Houses of Parliament:

> I said, by way of explanation, 'where the Prime Minister and government is' and Evita added 'Big Ben'. Gabby (4y 4m 27d) suddenly piped up: 'Peter Pan landed on Big Ben'.

With regard to technology:

> Gabby (4y 5m 17d) brought her iPad into the kitchen and said, 'It's a hundred – all filled up'. She meant fully charged, as shown by the symbol 100%.

After our trip to Australia, Gabby's interests turned to nature:

> Gabby asked me: 'What do long legs do?'
>
> Me: 'I don't know.'
>
> Gabby (4y 10m): 'What do they do in the garden?'
>
> Me: 'I don't know.'
>
> Gabby: 'They poo everywhere in the garden.'
>
> Me: 'Who told you that?'
>
> Gabby: 'My brain' (pointing at her head).

Links with Theory

Gabby was making all sorts of connections and was interested in everything she heard about and observed first-hand. She was finding out about technology by using her iPad and, occasionally, a computer. As someone who did not grow up with such sophisticated technology, I can see how important it is to have access and to learn through exploration. This is supported by most educators who believe in 'constructivism', defined by von Glasersfeld as the idea that 'knowledge could not be found ready made but must be constructed' by the learner (1995: 18). I do not believe that this idea is at odds with Vygotskian ideas about teaching, as Athey describes a 'constructivist teacher' as someone who takes into account what a child already knows (1990).

Reflections

Children's questions give us a window into their ideas about the world.

Do you have a way of recording children's questions?

Have you thought of using the questions children ask as a starting point for planning your curriculum?

Encouraging parents to share their children's questions with you can offer a rich topic for you to discuss with both the parents and the children.

SUMMARY

Gabriella's development and learning in her fifth year fell into five of the seven areas of the curriculum, as presented in the Early Years Foundation Stage Guidance document (DfE 2017). The three 'prime areas' are:

- physical development
- personal, social and emotional development
- communication and language.

And two of the specific areas are:

- mathematics including games with rules
- understanding the world – one of her 'puzzles' was 'falling in love' and 'getting married'.

As far as pedagogy is concerned:

Intent	Implementation	Impact
Supporting Gabby's physical development	Allowing and accompanying jumping on the bed with rhyme	Gabby develops strength in legs
Supporting her autonomy and creativity	Allowing her to create a soft room with cushions in our living room	She realizes her ideas are valued as well as physical development through more jumping
Creating opportunities for gross motor development	Taking her to different parks	She relishes physical challenges
Creating opportunities for Gabby's world to expand	Going on holidays to London, Latvia and Tenerife	She gains a wider view of the world
Keeping her safe	Setting boundaries, e.g. not leaning into plastic bag	She understands what is safe and unsafe

Intent	Implementation	Impact
Supporting her emotional development	Talking through incidents with her	She begins to understand herself and to verbally express how she is feeling
Helping her to understand mathematical concepts	Playing games with her and creating new games to play, e.g. with pick-n-sticks	She begins to understand quantity, one-to-one correspondence and equivalence
Supporting her language development	Telling her stories from books and orally	She is able to create her own stories and to tell them
Helping her learn about places	Buying a book about London in advance of their visit there	She is able to recognize landmarks
Helping her learn about history in a wide sense	Talking about events that are celebrated annually, e.g. Bonfire Night	She begins to understand the origins of some events

6   From 5 to 6 Years

Sadly, Gabriella's parents decided to separate during the year before her fifth birthday. Her father moved out shortly after Gabby's fifth birthday. Gabby's and Nicole's well-being was at the forefront of all of our minds at this time. We knew, as grandparents, that we could provide some stability, as we had done for our older grandchildren when their parents separated (Arnold 2003).

In addition, Gabby was moving into Year 1 at school, which was noticeably different from her Reception class area. Her school had prepared children well before the school holidays for the changes. Gabby was to have a male teacher and she was quite pleased about this. However, her new teacher went off sick after two weeks and subsequently left the school. Her class had a temporary teacher until Christmas and then a permanent teacher was appointed. These changes were unfortunate and added to Gabby's distress.

When I read through the diary for this year, Gabby obviously felt challenged at first, but her parents handled their separation as well as they could and she soon settled into the new arrangements. In light of these changes, and because I believe children's emotional well-being needs to be high for them to learn, I am going to begin this chapter with emotional development, followed by:

- questions
- history
- mathematical development
- language development.

Emotional Development

At the end of the section on emotions in Chapter 5, Gabby showed me that her toys were up in her mum's bedroom. A few days later:

Gabby (5y 2d) said, 'I sleep in Mummy's bedroom all of the time because my toys are up there. And Daddy sleeps in my bed'. I was brave enough to ask 'Why is that?'. Gabby responded with:

'Mummy and Daddy aren't getting on very well. They are arguing a lot'. When Gabby came out of school that day, she complained of a 'sore tummy' – I rubbed it for a while and she let me.

Just over a month later, the two girls and their dad came to our house for tea:

Near the time to go home, Gabby (5y 1m 4d) wanted 'two yollies'. We repeatedly said she could have one and then another one but she screamed and cried for two. I had to carry her to the car. It was only when I talked it through with Colette (my older daughter) that I realized it was not the 'yollies' but it was her mummy and daddy she wanted *together*.

Links with Theory

I viewed it as positive that Gabriella's parents had been honest and open with the two girls and that Gabby could understand and articulate what was happening, in terms of her parents not getting on very well.

However, getting used to the subsequent changes can still be difficult for children. My PhD focused on how children, in their play, work through issues to do with 'attachment' (Arnold 2007; Arnold and the Pen Green Team 2010). Whenever we experience change, I believe our attachment security is threatened. It is ironic that I did not immediately recognize that, when Gabriella wanted 'two yollies together', this was symbolic, and she was expressing that she wanted 'two parents' to be 'together'. I think I was too close to Gabby and too emotionally involved in making things OK for the family to see this until I was able to talk through what had happened.

Transitions

A couple of days after going back to school:

I looked after the two girls from 6.30am. Gabby (5y 2m 27d) took ages over breakfast and refused point blank to get dressed and started crying and screaming and saying 'I don't want to go to school. I hate school. I hate everything about school'. I reminded her that she'd enjoyed it last year. 'That was when I was four'. Eventually, I got her to school and she agreed that I could talk to her teacher about her not liking the much larger playground and that she needed someone to keep an eye on her. I spoke to Mr. Mc and (out of Gabby's earshot) said that there were changes at home too.

Later that day, I noted:

> I picked the girls up from school. Gabby was like a different person. She had told her friend 'Mr. Mc is keeping an eye on me'.
>
> Gabby had something to eat and drink and then said 'I'm going to play now. The point of coming here is to play'.

Two weeks later, her first teacher had left:

> Gabby (5y 3m 10d) did not want to go to school but went more readily because it was 'book and biscuit' day and I could go in and tell her a story along with other parents/carers. After the session, she did not want me to leave . . . I took her scooter when I went to pick her up and she was in good spirits. Again, when it was time for me to leave their house, she did not want me to leave.

Three days later:

> Paul and the two girls came around shortly after 10 and stayed till nearly 1pm when we were going to Georgia's for lunch. Gabby (5y 3m 13d) seemed really pleased at first but was 'on edge' emotionally and became distraught as soon as anything went wrong, e.g. dropping her glass of milk, which smashed on the kitchen floor . . . In between, she drew and played hopscotch in the garden, helped Pop cut the grass, watered the flowers and played dentists.

By this time, her father was living in a HMO (house of multiple occupancy) at the other end of town and he and the two girls were staying at our home when it was his weekend to care for the children (usually every other weekend).

Links with Theory

The move to Year 1 and to the much bigger playground seemed to add to Gabby's insecurity. I thought her remark that 'The point of coming here is to play' also revealed that she was missing the chance to play at school for most of the day and, being one of the younger children in her year, this was quite an adjustment too.

Gabby's desire for me not to leave her also indicated that she was less secure than usual (Bowlby 1997). When children are described as 'clingy', my reading of the situation, taking into account attachment theory, is that they feel insecure or threatened in some way and need extra reassurance (Arnold 2009). In the final observation in this section, Gabby was what my mother would have described as 'egg-shelly', rather fragile and needing a reason to cry. Gabby was sad; however, notice that the sadness did not last long. Soon after this, Gabby demonstrated her resilience and seemed to settle into their new routine.

> **Reflections**
>
> Many children live in reconstituted families.
>
> Are you aware of each child's family situation?
> Are you able to notice and comment on children's moods and emotions?
> Are you confident about sharing information with parents/ carers during times of transition?

Questions

Gabriella has always asked lots of questions but these seemed even more prolific and wide ranging during this year. Sometimes they seemed to come out of the blue, but at other times Gabby was using what she knew already and deducing something, which led to a question:

> I said I had been talking to my big brother on the phone and that he lived a long way away. Gabby (5y 1m 7d) asked, 'Does he speak English?'

On the same day:

> Gabby was looking at Pop's tablet dispenser. She referred to them as 'vitamins'. I said they were to keep his heart healthy because he has had a heart attack. Gabby obviously had not heard the term and asked 'When did he have the fight?' I explained that it was not a fight but an illness from which you can die and that, luckily, Pop has medicine to keep him well.

Sometimes, I went into long explanations that were unnecessary, such as later that day:

> Gabby asked 'Why is water wet?' – I explained about the three types of matter – and 'Where does water come from?'. I gave a long explanation about lakes, wells etc. but what Gabby meant was how did it get to the tap – i.e. by underground pipes to the bathroom.

Her final question on that day was:

What is an organization?

Gabriella was doing a maths calculation in her head and checking it out with me:

Gabby (5y 1m 29d) asked 'When Nicole is 26, will I be 22?' This followed on from a conversation we had had last week about Nicole being 4 years older than Gabby. She went through several examples, finishing with 'When Nicole is 25, will I be 21?' She also wanted to know how old Harry Styles was. We Googled and found out he was 23 – 1 year younger than her cousin Harry.

A few weeks later, I noticed her integrating some of this knowledge into her role play:

Gabby (5y 2m 27d) was playing going to the 'baby nest' to drop her baby off. She left 'big brother' (Teddy Tim) with me and said 'He's only six' . . . 'I'm 25 – I'm older than Harry'.

That same day, in the car going home:

Gabby asked, 'Why can't babies talk?' I explained that babies hear some language when they are in their mummies' tummies but after they're born they hear people talking all around them and, if they hear English, they learn English; if they hear Latvian, they learn to speak Latvian etc. Gabby then applied that to Russian and Polish and talked about her friend David's mum being Polish. I asked 'And his dad?' Gabby 'I think so'. Then added, 'Victor's mum was from the Ukraine but his dad was English'.

One day, we drove to East Carlton Park:

Gabby (5y 5m 7d) was interested in how far it was, so I measured it and told her: '2.9 miles from my house'. She wanted to know: 'How far will it be on the way back?'. At East Carlton, she noticed a tall tower with a clock 'like Big Ben' and mused, 'I wonder who lives in that big house?'.

Almost 3 months later, when Gabriella was 5y 8m 3d, we had another spate of questions:

'What are baby horses called?'

'Why are cows fat?'

'Why don't we ride lions?'

'Why do only boy lions have manes? Is it so we know who is the daddy? Is it so we know who is the mummy and who is the daddy? Even so the baby knows?'.

A few days later, Gabriella was still trying to work out who was older than who else in the family:

Gabby (5y 8m 11d) was looking at a photo and asked: 'So, is Eloise younger than Colette? And is Daddy younger than Colette? So you had Colette first?'.

Subsequently, the nature of her questions changed a bit:

Gabby (5y 11m 27d) asked: 'Do you know we live in Europe?'

Me: 'Yes.'

Gabby: 'I learned that at school today'. Then: 'Do you know that plural means more than one?'.

Links with Theory

Questions are by their nature significant and, coming from children, indicate the connections they are making in their thinking. The first one, about whether my brother speaks English, was understandable as Gabby has relatives in Latvia who do not speak English, so here she was making a connection between pieces of knowledge about family.

Nathan Isaacs focused on children's 'Why?' questions as an appendix to Susan Isaacs' book *Intellectual Growth in Young Children* (1930). He pointed out that children are building up a store of knowledge based on their experience. Often, 'Why?' questions occur because children discover they have a gap in knowledge, such as 'Why don't we ride lions?', or want an explanation of something that does not fit their previous experience. Children can become perturbed when something they discover does not fit with an assumption they have made, for example when Harry was 'put out' to discover his Nana, who was smaller in stature than his Grandmop, was nevertheless older. He thought that taller equals older (Arnold 2003).

The final two examples demonstrate a change, in the sense that Gabriella is asking whether I know some things she has learned at school.

> **Reflections**
> Teachers are encouraged to ask children open-ended questions.
>> Might it not be more productive if the questions came from children?
>> Gabby obviously relished the new information she was gaining. Would it be helpful to know some of what children share at home?

History

This section, although brief, shows some of the topics Gabriella was becoming interested in at school, as well as connections she was making about her own family history:

> In the car, Gabby (5y 3m 15d) asked me: 'Do you know about King John?' She told me the basic story and then we Googled him. Gabby told me, 'At first, he didn't want to sign the Magna Carta – he did it so his people would be loyal'. Then, looking at an image online: 'That's the sceptre. Where's the orb?' Followed closely by: 'Do you think William will be king?'.

Two months later, when we were at East Carlton Park:

> Gabby (5y 5m 7d) spotted the old train that has been painted and preserved and said, 'Daddy told me he used to climb on that when he was a little boy'.

> Gabby (5y 6m 3d) told me that Charles II was a king who liked parties. He was a 'fun' king. I mentioned Queen Victoria and her long reign, only superseded by Queen Elizabeth II, who, I reminded her, is 20 years older than me. (This conversation continues in the Maths section).

At 5y 8m 3d, a conversation about her next-door neighbour:

> led to a discussion about when Nicole joined their school. 'Did she start in Reception?' Me: 'No, she went straight into Year 2.' I had to explain that Nicole had been to Reception and Year 1 at a different school, like me when I came to Corby as an 8-year-old.

Links with Theory

History is very much about time, changes and significant events (Cooper 2002). These can be personal histories which, very much, form our identities, or historical figures like kings and queens. We can see from the small number of observations that Gabriella was interested in both, and could make some connections between past and present time and events.

The National Curriculum for Key Stage 1 history is fairly vague so, I think, developing chronological awareness and excitement and interest in history is most important at this stage. Opportunities to talk and write about historical figures can support other areas of the curriculum too (DfE, 2013).

Personally, I would like to see history in schools being a bit broader, reflecting children's heritages from their families' countries of origin.

Reflections

Think about how you can get children excited about the past.

You could begin with children's own stories of their families. What kinds of stories could you introduce? Which historical figures interest you?

Mathematics

What seemed really prevalent during this year was the sequencing or ordering of objects or events in Gabby's thinking. In earlier chapters, we saw how Gabby ordered or seriated objects in lines. She was learning the order of numbers up to 100, 'forwards and backwards' at school and this ordering showed up in many of our conversations (DfE 2013):

> Gabby sat on the kitchen side and smelt each essential oil. She said, 'Lemon is my favourite and orange is my second favourite' (although only first and second, Gabby (5y 2m 15d) is putting these in order).

Playing Snakes and Ladders:

> Last time we played, I had to tell Gabby which direction to go in when she moved her counter. This time, Gabby (5y 2m 27d) looked

at the number (if it was fairly small) and moved it in the right direction. If it was big, e.g. 78, she asked me what number it was and
then she decided which way she needed to move her counter.

She seemed interested in playing with numbers and 'seriating' anything she could find:

> Gabby (5y 3m 1d) spent some time with Pop in the garage using
> a tape measure, then the three of us played two games of
> Snakes and Ladders . . . a bit later, Gabby stacked the stacking
> beakers easily, selecting the right beaker to fit and explaining
> how she knew which to select. Then she used the weights from
> the bathroom and assigned the lightest to herself, the medium to
> me and the heaviest to Pop.

Gabby was also learning to 'count in multiples of twos, fives and
tens' at school and occasionally she practised this:

> Gabby (5y 3m 15d) counted in twos up to 26 (in the car coming
> home).

One morning we had a conversation on the way to school:

> Gabby (5y 4m 8d) was talking about birthdays and the fact that
> mine is next Monday. I said, 'Daddy's was in September'. Gabby
> said, 'My birthday was in June – first it was mine, then Anya's'.
> I added 'Yours is on the 11th and Anya's is on the 23rd.'

Gabby was very interested in birthdays, dates and ages:
    Gabby (5y 4m 22d) said 'I'm going to Charlie's party on the 8th of
November. Today is the 2nd of November . . . 3rd, 4th, 5th, 6th, 7th,
8th . . . not very long to his party'. Went on to ask, 'How come when
you were 69, Pop was 70?' I explained his birthday is in March and
mine is October, so for a few months it might seem that he is a year
older than me. Gabby: 'But you're both 71 now?' Me: 'Yes.' Gabby:
'71 or 17?' Me 'I could be 17 but then I wouldn't have any children or
gorgeous grandchildren.' That led to questions about how old I was
when I had each of our three children – '21 – Colette; 24 – Paul and
27 – Eloise'.
There was a development when, at 5y 4m 24d, she:

> played Snakes and Ladders several times, mostly beating me.
> Can now predict – 'I don't want to get a three' (as I'll go down a
> snake) or 'I need a two' (to go up a ladder).

Looking forward to special events helped:

> Gabby (5y 5m 13d) is very excited about going to Cadbury World tomorrow and seeing Santa. She talked about other things that happen at other times of the year: 'October – Halloween; June – her birthday; January – Nicole's, Georgia's and Mummy's birthdays'. I added 'October' and she said 'Mop's, Robin's (their cat) and Rhys' birthdays'. (Rhys is her cousin, born in Australia, and 4 years younger than her. He shares a birthday with Robin.)

Gabriella continued to have many conversations about locating events in time:

> Gabby (5y 5m 16d): 'When Pop is 72, you will be 71 until October because his birthday is in March and that comes before October'. Then mentioned my brother's granddaughter whose birthday is in the September before Gabby's, which is in June: 'When I'm 6, Autumn will still be 6'.

Remembering that I had told her that the Queen is 20 years older than me:

> Gabby (5y 6m 3d) 'You are 71 and the Queen is 91' and other examples up to, 'When you are 80, the Queen will be 100 . . . and then she'll die'. I said that no-one knows when they will die. That morning, Gabriella had the Latvian game Cirks (Circus) set up for us to play. I won the first game and I said, 'You have to learn to lose as well as win'. She said, '*I KNOW!*' (I think she's heard that before). We played dominoes next and she won.

It was nearing Christmas so I helped Nicole and Gabriella make and ice a Christmas cake. Gabby took great care. A few days later, we played bingo, as Gabriella had learned to play it at school. On Christmas Day:

> Gabby (5y 6m 14d) got a watch (among many other presents) and has just realized that when her watch shows, for example, 9 o'clock, so does the clock and everyone else's watch (haven't introduced time zones yet!).

Nicole had Heelys and Gabby was desperate for a pair too. Having gone ice skating over Christmas, she was sure she could skate:

> Gabby (5y 6m 22d) reported: 'Mummy found Heelys that are size 12 – I am size 9, then 10, 11, 12 . . .'

The same day:

> Gabby counted in twos to 100 and in fives to 100 (it was not yet automatic – there were pauses, especially before 30, 40 etc., but all were correct).

Gabriella was still interested in 'ordering' objects:

> Gabby (5y 7m 2d) lined up eight small bottles of essential oil in order of preference after reading each label and smelling each one. When Pop came in, she asked him to do the same.

We went on holiday to India for four weeks and the conversations about ages and time continued on our return:

> Gabby (5y 10m) said, 'You're 71 and Pop is 71'. I replied, 'Pop is 72 because he had his birthday while we were in India'. Gabby: 'Ahh – then you'll be 72 when it's your birthday'. . . A bit later, I reminded Gabby that 'We go to Center Parcs in just over two weeks'. Gabby: 'It's the 11th today', thought for a minute and then went upstairs to look at Nicole's calendar – came to the top of the stairs and called down '16 days!' (Gabby seems to be grasping the concept of time. Knows all the family birthdays and when they are).

Pic 6.1 Gabby lined up essential oils in order of preference

Pop posed a question:

> At dinner, we were talking about ages. Pop said, 'I'm 72 and, when you're 6, how much older will I be than you?' Gabby (5y 11m 13d) thought carefully, really concentrating, and said '66'.

At 5y 11m 20d, Gabby was in hospital for the day with a racing heartbeat, which has happened occasionally since. We are not sure why. A week later, we were at the park:

> Gabby repeatedly climbed up a metal slide. It took a lot of effort and she repeated this in multiples of six at least six times. She got faster and finally asked me to time her – it took 32 seconds for her to climb up and slide down six times.

Links with Theory

Gabriella loves games and played Snap for a long time before moving on to more complex games. Whereas in Snap you match symbols, other games she played used equivalence and ordering. According to Haylock and Cockburn (2013): 'Much of mathematics . . . is concerned with recognizing and applying equivalences and transformations' (p.18). Gabby clearly practised using equivalences when playing Snakes and Ladders (dots on the dice equalled the number of moves) and, eventually, could predict the number on the dice she wanted to avoid or throw.

Gabby was also becoming very familiar with the 'ordinal aspect' of numbers (first, second, third and so on) up to 100, when playing Snakes and Ladders and the Latvian game Cirks (Circus). Her very strong interest in ages was also about the ordinal aspect, but was further complicated by the order of the months, which she also seemed to be mastering at this time. However, when she counted the days to Charlie's birthday, she used the ordinal aspect to calculate the 'cardinal aspect' (quantity) – how many days to Charlie's birthday party? (Haylock and Cockburn 2013: 32). Similarly, when I mentioned our forthcoming trip to Center Parcs, Gabby counted how many days there were on the calendar until the day we were going.

Gabby used 'transformation' when she calculated her and Nicole's future ages and also mine and the Queen's future ages. She was adept at adding on, for example, 9 years to the Queen's age and 9 years to my age, so the comparison looked different (or transformed) but the difference was the same.

Finally, Gabby subtracted her 6 years from Pop's 72 years in her head.

Reflections

It can be really helpful to know what calculations children are making at home when it comes to learning mathematics in settings.

> Think about the sorts of questions you could ask parents/ carers in order to learn about children's interests and number knowledge.
> What could you display in your setting to engage children with numbers?

Language Development

Role playing at our house continued and became more complex. Sometimes we were certain Gabby was re-enacting what had happened at school. For example:

> Gabby (5y 4m 11d) asked Pop to copy a sentence. She was 'teacher'. She then 'marked' his work using colour-coded highlighters to mark up what was correct or in error. Pop deliberately did not use a capital letter at the beginning of the sentence but put one in the sentence. Gabby picked up on both errors and told Pop he needed to practise. Later, Gabby played a similar game with Paul.

Gabby continued to enjoy and initiate games. In this instance, it was 'hiding the dice':

> Gabby (5y 4m 19d) found a really good hiding place in the computer room. It took me quite a while to find – when I was very close (or 'warmer', as we were in the habit of saying), she said, 'You're on fire!' (I had not heard her use that expression before). Played on the computer with Pop writing sentences, e.g. 'Pop is not a poo. Robin is a good cat.' (She tried to write 'black and white cat' – we could see what she meant although the spelling was not accurate – we did not correct it). Played games like Obb and Bob and matching words to pictures. Nicole promoted her to Level 3 but she could pretty much work out each word.

Pic 6.2 Gabby drew her cat Robin using a new technique (5y 1m 3d)

At times, Gabby wanted to practise her schoolwork, for example:

> Gabby (5y 4m 23d) wanted to practise her spellings. She asked me to test her on this week's spellings. She was pretty good at crossing out and writing the correct version. 'Light' was difficult – she tended to get the 'g' and 'h' the wrong way around first time. She went on to try out the next couple of weeks' spellings and, eventually, to try out writing with her eyes closed.

Gabby still used 'pretend writing' in some role play situations that she created, for example when we played shops at her house:

> Gabby (5y 5m 5d) was the shopkeeper and I was the customer. I had to find real things to buy in her bedroom. I would ask 'How much?' and she said an amount, e.g. '99 60' and I said, 'That's a lot' and she said, 'I can give it cheaper'. Sometimes, she went to look up the price in a book – flicked through pages and 'wrote' using very fast pretend writing. Also asked 'Cash or card?' when it came to paying. When I paid by card, she said 'I have to do something' and keyed in some numbers before I put in my 'number'.

It is a tradition in our family to go to a pantomime near Christmas, so we went with Paul, Nicole and Gabby to see *Cinderella* at Milton

Pic 6.3 Gabby practising her spellings

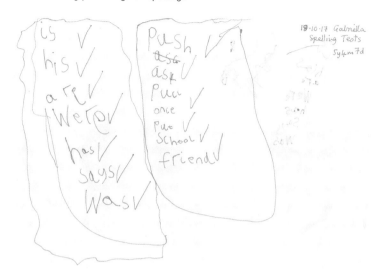

Keynes that Christmas. Since their parents have separated, they go to two pantomimes each Christmas and sometimes compare them.

Gabriella's reading was coming on. The day after our panto trip:

> Gabby read *The Tiger Who Came to Tea* (a favourite story) spontaneously and only stumbled over a few words.

Gabby was becoming interested in words and meanings and, at 5y 6m 22d, she reported:

> There are two words for 'cock' (I think she means two meanings of the word) – one is a swear word – 'cock' for cock a doodle doo, what hens do, and the other 'cock' is willy. Daddy says I can only say 'cock a doodle doo'.

Gabby was being my 'teacher':

> Gabby (5y 7m 2d) is setting, correcting and marking my work. She is doing pretend writing in between, which she says, is the 'blue dot challenge', which she, as a teacher, 'needs to show the headteacher . . .'

> After lunch, Paul was teasing her by saying, 'You're as big as a bourbon . . . You're as brown as a bourbon' etc. (her favourite

biscuits). Gabby responded by asking, 'Are you using similes?'. . . Later on, Gabby referred to a 'diffuser' in our living room
as a 'confuser' and then laughed and corrected herself.

At her home the following day:

We were having a conversation about fog. I asked Gabby if she
knew what fog is. She explained, 'Fog is like a cloud on the
ground instead of in the sky'. She said she learned that from
Peppa Pig.

We were just back from four weeks in India, when Paul, Nicole and
Gabriella spent the afternoon at our home:

Gabby (5y 9m 19d) played with baby, buggy and teddy . . . Initiated a game of 'dentist's' with me, which was brief – she looked
in my mouth using a torch, got an empty pill dispenser and put
pretend tablets in my mouth. Then wanted Pop to play 'This is
the way the lady rides'; also lots of tickling and noisy kisses
(zubberts) . . .

Initiated a game of 'doctors' with Paul. She was the patient with
a sore leg, so she could not walk. This game went on for a while.
She had a walking stick, went for an x-ray, had different treat-
ments and went to a 'special hospital'.

Gabby (5y 11m 13d) was very excited about her tooth falling out and
about becoming 6 soon. It was Thursday and we were having dinner:

Gabby told us she had a certificate from school saying she can
sit at the 'golden table' tomorrow for lunch and she can invite a
friend. She said she was going to ask Jay but has not told him
yet as she may change her mind. Pop teased her, saying
he wanted to be her guest. In the end, she said to Pop, 'Oh,
it's not tomorrow, it's Monday', whispering to me 'It's really
tomorrow' . . . A bit later, the news was on TV and Gabby recognized 'Theresa May, the Prime Minister' and talked about 'taxes
going in a big pot to help everyone' (we were surprised Gabby
had a grasp of that concept).

Links with Theory

Gabriella continued to engage in pretend play and, as devoted grandparents, we were her play partners when she was with us. Lake and

Evangelou (2019: 221) recommend that there are 'benefits of adults engaging in children's pretend play'. Inevitably, we added new vocabulary although Gabby was always leading in terms of themes.

The same could be said of our conversations, which were usually initiated by Gabby and lasted as long as she was interested. You can see from the observations here that Gabby was engaged in learning spellings and grammar at school and that she was keen to practise, either formally, as with her spellings, or more informally by playing 'teacher' to adult members of the family (DfE 2013). Gabby even picked up on the fact that her father was using 'similes', defined as 'a figure of speech comparing one thing to another' (Collins 2006: 698).

Following on from information gathered by Piaget during 'clinical interviews' with children, it was Margaret Donaldson (1987) who taught us the importance of context and that situations need to make 'human sense' to children (p.24).

Gabby used her first-hand experiences symbolically when engaging in role play and gradually acquired new language, as well as a deeper understanding of each situation.

Reflections

It would be impossible, because of ratios of adults to children in a setting, to become as involved as we were, as grandparents, in a child's play. However, perhaps by collecting play themes from children and families, popular role play situations could be set up.
 What other ways could you support language in your setting?

SUMMARY

This year began a little shakily for Gabriella, so supporting her emotional development was at the forefront of our minds. Hence, the themes for this year from 5 to 6 years old are:

- emotional development – coping with changes at home and school
- questions, which were wide ranging
- history – learned at school and at home
- mathematical development
- language development.

As far as pedagogy was concerned:

Intent	Implementation	Impact
Supporting Gabby's emotional development	Talking to her teacher and asking him to keep an eye on Gabby in the playground	Gabby feels cared for and thought about at school
Expanding her knowledge of the world	Responding to her questions	She grows in confidence in relation to what she knows about
Expanding her knowledge of her family	Patiently responding to questions repeatedly asked about birthdays and ages	She integrates some of the information about ages into her role play
Supporting and expanding her wider knowledge of history	Listening to her interests and Googling for further information alongside her	She gains more general knowledge of history and learns how to research questions that interest her
Increasing her mathematical knowledge	Playing games with her, responding to specific questions and, occasionally, posing questions	She adds to her knowledge about seriating and ordering up to 100, can locate events in time and begins to understand duration (time)
Increasing her vocabulary	Taking part in role play and introducing language in context	She increases her vocabulary and her understanding of certain social situations
Supporting her learning of spellings and grammar	Testing her on her spellings at her request and playing the role of 'pupil' to her 'teacher'	She consolidates her learning about sentence formation and spellings
Expanding her knowledge of narrative	Telling stories; going to shows/films; watching films on TV	She begins to tell, read and write stories

7 From 6 to 7 Years

This was the year when Gabriella really flourished at school. She had a circle of friends and one special best friend, Remie. By now she was a proficient swimmer, having attended weekly swimming lessons at the local pool. She also began attending a music school each Saturday to learn to play the guitar and recorder initially. Later, she switched to guitar and singing and studied the piano and drums at school.

Her father bought his own flat a couple of months after Gabby's sixth birthday, quite near to where we live, so the girls were able to stay overnight at his place, but I was still taking them to school some days and they visited us regularly for meals and to play.

The main area of development that I noticed in the data was conceptual development. Sometimes this related to mathematical development and sometimes to language development or both and I hope to show how some of the knowledge is underpinned by previous experiences and actions. I will begin with a reminder of some of the theory, so this chapter covers:

- theory that links language with concepts
- language and literacy
- mathematics.

Theory that Links Language with Concepts

I want to draw attention to some of the early years literature and a strong finding about conceptual development. A 'concept' is difficult to define as it is not an object but an idea and can be quite abstract. Teaching complex concepts like 'time' or 'age' is tricky. However, Athey (1990: 14) pointed out that 'basic concepts are formed between the ages of two and five'. Athey was referring to the repeated actions or 'schemas' that children spontaneously carry out in order to understand the world around them. She thought of these actions as 'partial concepts' that gradually co-ordinate and that children abstract from in order to understand more complex concepts and ideas. Often, we recognize the repeated actions but are not sure how to support them. Athey (2007: 42) recommends 'helping the child to become more conscious of the "doing'". We do this by accompanying the action with language describing the action.

Matthews (2003: 29), drawing on more recent research on the brain, informs us that the word(s) acts as a 'pivot' in the brain so that it holds experiences together to form concepts. For example, when Gabby was almost two and transporting beads from the conservatory to the garden to make a 'line' of beads, I said to her: 'I can see you carrying beads and making a line', then on subsequent occasions, 'making that line' became a partial concept and that could be applied in a more abstract way to, for example, the months of the year or the temporal succession of birthdays in our family, as we have seen in the longitudinal study of Gabby.

More recent research carried out by Atherton and Nutbrown (2013) recommends 'tuning in conceptually' and using the 'language of form' (p.37). By 'form', they mean schemas or repeated actions. A child is looking to see what the materials 'afford' that matches their current interest and, as adults, we need to observe carefully in order to tune in to that interest and use the language that matches their actions (Gibson 1986). In a further study, Brierley and Nutbrown refer to this as 'schematic pedagogy' (2017). It is primarily about 'hearing language that matches their intent' (Brierley and Nutbrown 2017: 135). If a close match is made, the child is more likely to remember and internalize that language and concept. Children seem to recognize when this 'match' is made by looking very pleased because they realize that they are leading their own learning and we, as adults, tune in to their intentions by paying close attention.

Language and Literacy

Words and Creative Role Play

Gabby (6y 6d) and Nicole were staying with us for the weekend after her birthday and we went to the Riverside Hub indoor play centre as a birthday treat:

> Gabby loved laser tag, go-karts and soft play. We had a conversation about cancer and heart disease. Pop explained about stents. Gabby wanted to know, 'What is "numb"?'
>
> Later, at the boating lake park, Gabby asked, 'What is "hefty"?' (We were not sure where she had come across this word). . .
>
> We had fun talking about Pop's report from hospital referring to a 'well-nourished man'. Gabby immediately caught on that this meant 'plump' or 'chubby'.

Later on, at home:

> Gabby and I played dentists, which developed into a role play about stealing tablets and the police (me) chasing Gabby. When I caught up with her, she said that her friend Nicole had stolen them and given them to her and that she did not realize they were stolen!

Links with Previous Experiences and/or Theory

By now Gabby was reading a lot more and coming across new words about which she was curious. The conversation about stents and how they are inserted (either through the groin or wrist) was important as, a few weeks later, Gabby had to wear a heart monitor, following on from her racing heartbeat. Pop was explaining that, when stents are fitted, the area is 'numb' so you are not in pain. On the day the monitor was being fitted:

> Gabby (6y 2m 17d) asked me 'Do they have to cut you open to fit the heart monitor?' (gesturing to her chest). I said 'Absolutely not'.

It may be difficult, as a child, to imagine how your heart (deep inside you) can be monitored without intrusion.

The role play about stealing tablets, which began as usual, turned into something fictional beyond Gabby's experience. This was really the first time I noticed her take her narrative in a completely unexpected direction, although she used humour frequently in conversation and the fact that 'her friend' (who was in the wrong) was called Nicole (the same name as her sister) was, I think, her way of bringing humour into the story. Although the National Curriculum has a strong emphasis on spelling, punctuation and grammar, it also mentions drama and states that 'pupils should be able to adopt, create and sustain a range of roles' (DfE 2013: 14). However much training or teaching children are offered about writing, I believe that writing begins with talking and acting and this, too, is emphasized in the curriculum document.

Reading and Writing

Paul, Nicole and Gabby (6y 3m 26d) popped in:

> Paul said Gabby read three books this morning and is becoming more fluent as a reader. Nicole said she wanted to put them down in Gabby's reading diary (from school) but Gabby did not want her to do that. I hope that is a development in two ways: (1) Fluency,

which makes reading more pleasurable and less formulaic, and (2) Being intrinsically motivated to read, not because of an extrinsic reward, but purely for pleasure.

Gabby's writing was developing too:

Paul told me Gabby's teacher had shown him one-and-a-half pages of writing Gabby had done on tsunamis, hurricanes and volcanoes and said, 'This is what we'd expect in Year 3' . . . I commented, 'Maybe you'll write books like me when you grow up?' Gabby looked surprised. I reminded her that I had written four books and she said, 'You'll have to ask *permission*' (if I included her in a future book).

Nicole and Gabby (6y 6m 24d) came for tea with Paul:

Gabby read four pages of a David Walliams book to me (*Mr. Stink*). There were lots of long words, many of which she knew.

Links with Previous Experiences and/or Theory

Being intrinsically motivated links with the idea of 'involvement' and too many extrinsic rewards, unconnected to the activity in hand, can dampen children's enthusiasm (Donaldson 1987).

Pic 7.1 A birthday card to Mop (6y 4m 10d)

Pic 7.2 Gabby designed a Christmas card (6y 5m 29d)

Gabby had experience of giving written permission when I wrote a journal article about her language linked to schemas that year (Arnold 2018). I also made the two girls photo books of their school holidays but did not include pictures of their cousins as, I explained, I had not asked their permission. This prompted Gabby to sometimes refuse permission and I think this was to test out whether I was being authentic in seeking her permission.

Researching

Gabby (6y 9m 7d) was very excited that her caterpillars had arrived:

> Gabby got Nicole's homemade book out about the transformation of caterpillars to butterflies. She was not keen on the page where the red liquid came from the butterfly – thought it was blood, but was much happier when we looked it up and found it was 'meconium', defined as 'what the butterfly does not need that was part of the caterpillar' . . . Gabby drew a butterfly and went on to draw a spider, bee and pig (which she said Nicole had shown her how to draw).

Links with Previous Experiences and/or Theory

This is where Gabriella's sociocultural context (her sister, Nicole's experiences) seemed to influence her. Nicole was very interested in the transformation from caterpillar to butterfly from the age of four

and, having experienced the process in her Reception class, had caterpillars at our home one year and subsequently at their home, as well as
photographing and making a book about the process. In this instance,
I could deduce that Nicole led Gabby's learning (Vygotsky 1978).
Gabby also acknowledged that Nicole had shown her how to draw a
spider, bee and pig. These were also strong interests of Nicole's.

More than 2 years after these observations were made, Gabriella
(now 8 years old) sent us a PowerPoint presentation she had just
made, entitled 'My Butterfly Project', documenting the transformation from caterpillars to butterflies that summer. In it, she mentions
'meconium' and understands what it is.

Being Teacher

Gabby's role play continued and became more complex as she
taught me to write sentences and correct my mistakes:

> Gabby told me, 'You're in Year 2 now so you need to expand
> nouns and use suffix endings'. She gave me the following words
> to which I had to add either –ness or –ment:
>
> fresh, ill, kind, refresh, confine, good, bad.
>
> During the 'lesson' I had to go to the toilet and Gabby threatened to
> shorten my break by 10 minutes if I was too long. I shouted from
> the loo that I was doing a poo so she said I could have a bit longer.

Pic 7.3 Making a book at Mop's (6y 10m)

Links with Previous Experiences and/or Theory

I imagine this is lifted straight from a lesson at school and that, as a teacher, she is aware of setting boundaries with her pupils.

Devising Games with Language

While playing in our garden:

> Gabby (6y 11m 21d) developed a game of throwing a ball to the other player over the washing line and then, as each person threw, they had to state a fact. She gave an example: 'When we breathe out, we produce carbon dioxide – the flowers eat it and then produce oxygen, which we breathe in!'

It was the day before Gabriella's seventh birthday. Nicole was ill so Paul and Gabby came for tea:

> Gabby and Paul played with the farm. The two animals (the cow was called Moo) left and then came back 'to take over the farm'; in fact, she said they 'might take over the world!'

> Gabby liked her cake but said she had never had a 'cake from Asda before'. One of the first things she said was 'Can I take a piece home for Nicole?'.

Links with Previous Experiences and/or Theory

I am not sure whether the game with the washing line was taken straight from a game played at school. It seems likely. Again, she used humour by suggesting that a cow 'might take over the farm or even the world' when playing with the animals. Gabby's experience of birthday cakes is rather individual so she may be comparing them with the cake from Asda we bought to acknowledge her forthcoming birthday.

Mathematics

Voting

Evita's uncle had died, so the two girls stayed with us for three nights while their mum went to Latvia for the funeral. The weather was lovely so we played outdoors most of the time. We decided to go out for dinner and Gabby suggested '*voting*' on where to go as we did not all agree.

Links with Previous Experiences and/or Theory

Gabby (6y 27d) clearly understood what voting means, so I have been thinking about how she 'internalized' that knowledge. Voting clearly involves a one-to-one correspondence (that is, each person has one vote), counting the number of votes, and the deciding factor being the bigger total. I think the many games of Snakes and Ladders may have contributed, because you use one-to-one correspondence to move the counter one square for each dot on the dice, and you also count the number of moves and the first to reach the 100th square is the winner. Gabby also occasionally played raffles, where tickets were distributed to each member of the family and she drew out a winner. In this instance, there were five of us so, if we had two restaurants in mind, there could be a clear winner.

Making a Choice

Gabby often looked at essential oils at our home:

> Gabby (6y 2m 9d) sorted out the essential oils. She smells each one, reads the name and then selects or rejects. She put to one side lime and blood orange and said, 'I'm going to make my *final* choice'. She chose lime, saying, 'I *usually* go for blood orange'.

Similarly, later on,

> Gabby sorted the buttons – made a line of her 'favourites' and put them in a separate bag.

Links with Previous Experiences and/or Theory

These sorts of play link closely with the lining up and seriating that Gabby was doing with objects from she was very young (Athey 1990: 42). As well as seriating in order of preference, she was also 'classifying' or grouping certain buttons as her 'favourites' and separating them from the tin of buttons (Gruber and Voneche 1977). These processes were becoming more refined, as shown in the use of Gabriella's language 'a *final* choice', implying that she was choosing those oils she liked, and then deciding which was her absolute favourite on this occasion. Gabriella also contrasted this choice with what she had chosen as favourite on many other occasions. This involves a sense of number – the amount of times she had chosen blood orange compared with the one time she chose lime.

Time

That same day, we were talking about the essential oils we had bought with a diffuser as a gift for Paul. We had bought him olbas, lavender and tea tree. I said I would try to get him some lemon, lime and blood orange (Gabby's favourites). I said I had bought them in Australia:

> Gabby said jokingly, 'Go to Australia for some more'. I said, 'You know it takes all day to get to Australia – it's a 20 hour flight!' Gabby corrected me: '20 hours is not all day – a day is 24 hours'. Went on to discuss how long it might take by boat. Gabby was surprised that people used to take 6 weeks: 'The whole of the summer holiday!'.

Links with Previous Experiences and/or Theory

Gabby had already established that time/duration can feel like a relative concept – that is, 2 minutes cleaning your teeth seems to be a long time but 2 minutes before leaving home seems like a short time, even though the duration is the same.

Now she had the idea or concept of a day but was a little inflexible in how it is measured, as she had been taught that a day is 24 hours (correctly, I might add). Vygotsky talks about 'spontaneous concepts' connecting with 'scientific concepts' as taught in school (1986: 271). This is a good example. Gabriella had a sense of what a day is from her first-hand experience of day and night but she had been taught in school that a day is 24 hours. It is as if those two bits of information are not yet quite connecting, hence her inflexibility. Much of her role play was about night (when the light was 'enveloped') and day. According to Athey, '*Time* and *distance* have their origins in early *trajectories*' (1990: 193). The lining up of objects and then the sequencing of events contributes to the concept of time. As adults, we create timelines and Gantt charts to symbolize the completion of projects and to make the abstract concepts visible on paper or screen. We have seen in the last couple of chapters Gabby's interest in the sequencing of events.

Queuing

Three days later, we went to Fermyn Woods Country Park. Most popular was the zipline:

> Gabby (6y 2m 12d) did not go on at first, as it looked too daunting (the launch spot seemed very high). Finally, she plucked up the courage and then went on several times. We went to the café for lunch and I told Gabriella she could go on again after lunch. As we approached, I said, 'There's a long queue for the zipline now'. Gabby said 'That's OK – I'll get a turn *eventually*'.

Links with Previous Experiences and/or Theory

I thought her use of 'eventually' needed unpicking. Obviously, we can see the line and we can subtract one person at a time from that line until they have all had a go. This was a little like Gabby subtracting (in her head) her 6 years from Pop's 72 years in Chapter 6. Haylock and Cockburn (2013) outline several 'subtraction stories' that can help children grasp subtraction (p.69). In this instance, Gabriella could see that there was a long queue and this was equivalent to a long wait for a turn but she knew she would get a turn eventually.

Classifying

As we saw earlier, Gabby classified some buttons as her 'favourites'. On another occasion:

> Gabby (6y 2m 17d) played with the buttons and devised a game whereby she picked out two and said 'Guess which is *rare*?' I would point at one and she would say whether it was rare or not. I asked, 'How do you know?' and Gabby replied, 'I just know if there's much of one and not so much of the other'. I explained that we say 'many' if talking about discrete objects (such as buttons) but 'much' if we speak of materials, e.g. cornflour.

Links with Previous Experiences and/or Theory

Gabby seemed to know precisely what 'rare' meant and, again, it was to do with quantity and making comparisons between two amounts. In this case, it was probably not necessary to count unless there looked to be similar amounts, but, after all her practice counting in games, this was easy by now. She had continued to play Snakes and Ladders and Ludo, as well as 'Game of Life', which involves stars, money and forfeits and is fairly complicated.

More Research

I had put a cloth bag containing six bead bracelets in the toybox. I imagined that, when Gabriella discovered them, it might prompt some sort of dressing up and role play. I was so wrong:

> Gabby (6y 9m 14d) noticed the bag containing six bracelets. She lined them up on the carpet, and, firstly, showed me each one in turn and asked me whether I liked it. She was beginning to

research which was my favourite. Then she replaced them in the line, wrote a list and added '/20'. She asked me to give each a score out of 20 and the reasons for my score. When it came to my obvious favourite, I gave it 18/20 but she skilfully persuaded me that if it was the one I liked best I ought to give it 20/20.

Links with Previous Experiences and/or Theory

This resonated with 'ranking' objects in order of preference, and also with the idea of 'voting' for which bracelet I liked best. This links with the teaching of statistics, which is part of the Year 2 curriculum (DfE 2013: 112). This took 'seriating' to a new level. We saw Gabby 'seriating' in a simpler way in earlier chapters, for example

Pic 7.4 Choosing my favourite bracelet – marks out of 20

in Chapter 3, when she lined up pastry cutters in order of size and attributed each to a person.

Making Predictions

We saw earlier that Gabriella enjoyed predicting and comparing ages. The following conversation began with Nicole asking 'Are we going to Center Parcs?'. Nicole wanted to know what it would cost.

> This led to Nicole asking: 'Who will get your stuff when you die?' I explained that it would be shared between our three children. Nicole asked 'What about me?' I responded: 'Only if your daddy dies'. Gabby (6y 10m 13d) chipped in: 'I'll probably be 15 when you die and Nicole will be . . . (worked it out) 19' (not sure if Gabby thinks this is the far distant future) and added, 'She (Nicole) might have a car'.

Links with Previous Experiences and/or Theory

So this was an extension of 'When Nicole is x age, I will be y age'? In this instance, Gabby was trying to predict a particular event in relation to their ages and, considering I will be 80 when Gabby is 15, it could be a reasonable prediction that I might die. Age is acknowledged to be a tricky concept for children to grasp (Gruber and Voneche 1977). One concept that Gabby had been working on extensively is 'temporal succession'. Many children of around her age, when asked about who was born before whom in the family, show confusion and equate height with age as Harry did when he was younger (Gruber and Voneche 1977: 567; Arnold 2003). It strikes me as a sort of 'conservation' problem in the sense that the difference between the two ages is constant or 'conserved' as long as the number of years added on to each is equal, so, as time passes, it passes equally for all involved.

Reflections

Do you note down the use of fresh conceptual language as I have here, e.g. abstract ideas such as 'eventually', 'voting and 'transformation'?

How do you think children learn concepts?

How can you help children to learn about abstract concepts such as 'time'?

SUMMARY

This chapter charts the development of some concepts. They are organized under:

- theory that links language with concepts
- language and literacy
- mathematics.

As far as pedagogy is concerned:

Intent	Implementation	Impact
Helping Gabby extend her language and understanding	Engaging in a conversation about heart procedures	Gabby increases her understanding that feeling can be 'numb' when a procedure is carried out
Encouraging her creative role play	Taking part in her storyline	She experiments with creating fiction
Making her aware of possible future aspirations	Having a conversation about being an author	Her aspirations increase
Making her aware that her permission is part of the process	Talking about permissions and asking her permission regularly	She exercises choice and sometimes refuses permission
Supporting her ideas	Taking part in games she has devised	Her self-esteem increases and her language and ideas are extended
Extending her understanding of time	Engaging in a conversation about travelling to Australia by plane and ship	Extends her knowledge of duration
Supporting her calculation of her age 'when I die' and acknowledging that I will die	Engaging in a conversation about how old Nicole and Gabby will be when I die	Gabby consolidates some of her ideas about predicting and death

Concluding Thoughts

Strands That Run through the Whole Story

1 Supporting the '**emotional well-being**' of Gabby and her sister
is a thread that runs through from before birth until the present
time and into the future. This was supported by her parents,
extended family and professionals like her two family workers
at nursery and her teachers at school. Laevers' work on well-being, as well as firmly established concepts like 'attachment theory', helped me to think about Gabby's well-being each day and
also how to support her through transitions and change (Laevers
1997; Bowlby 1997). The Leuven well-being signals are very use-
ful, both to professionals and to parents and carers, in helping us
to notice when a child's well-being is a bit lower than usual.
Within families, we can usually identify the cause but that may
be a bit more difficult in settings, which is why relationships with
families are crucial, especially during a child's early years (Whalley and the Pen Green Team 2017).

2 **Relationships** were a second strand that ran through Gabby's
story, often providing a 'secure base' (Bowlby 1997: 209) so that
Gabby could explore and take risks in her development and
learning. Friendships with adults outside her family and with
other children were and continue to be important to Gabby
(Trevarthen 2002). I find emotional well-being and relationships to be the foundation on which all development and learning builds. Again, 'attachment theory' helped me to understand
what was happening when Gabby trusted those people close to
her and when she felt slightly threatened by people she was less
familiar with (Bowlby 1997). Relationships, particularly with
friends and with her older sister Nicole, often enabled Gabby to
reach her 'zone of proximal development', as described by
Vygotsky (1978).

3 **Communication** enabled Gabby to develop and learn, from her
early gestures, to which we responded, to her well-developed
sense of humour, which enables her to tease even elderly adults
in the family. Conversations initiated by Gabby were and continue to be important. Research by Trevarthen indicates that

babies are born looking to communicate and, as a family, we recognized this urge (Trevarthen et al. 2018a) and responded thoughtfully. There is also evidence that schemas and language link (Arnold 2018), so we tuned in to Gabby's interests conceptually. Therefore, we used language to comment on her actions, which matched her conceptual concerns (Atherton and Nutbrown 2013; Brierley and Nutbrown 2017). Consequently, Gabby demonstrated her understanding through the language she was using (Arnold 2018).

4 **Schemas leading to conceptual understanding** run through this story, from the urge to perform up/down movements (Chapter 1) to understanding the concept of 'lived age' (Chapter 6). Gabby demonstrated an interest in a cluster of schemas that I recorded from early on. Additionally, we noticed when something new caught her eye, for example objects that rotate, towards the end of her first year (Athey 2007), which contributed to her existing cluster of schemas. As we noticed this, we were able to feed the new interest. Her mother also noticed one of her first schematic co-ordinations of containing and trajectory, again towards the end of her first year. This was significant because Gabby could now have a different impact on the objects she was interacting with. Here, she brought together 'two separate aspects of knowing' (Athey 1990: 37). It is through the co-ordination of schemas that children are able to develop their conceptual understanding. We know that supporting her explorations has resulted in sound knowledge and understanding across subject areas, as well as a thirst for knowledge.

5 Gabby's **persistence and resilience** show how she rose to demands from physical challenges, such as going on a high slide, and to emotional challenges, such as moving up in school and losing her teacher. Dweck recognized that 'learning goals' encourage 'mastery', whereas 'performance goals' can result in giving up and a kind of 'helpless' attitude (Dweck and Leggett 1988). Gabby does not usually give up easily and the disposition to persevere will stand her in good stead throughout her education and in life (Carr et al. 2009).

6 Our grandparent **pedagogy** also runs through the book. I choose 'pedagogy' rather than 'teaching' as, at all times, we encouraged Gabby to lead her own learning. Our style was always supportive rather than directive and the learning occurred because we

'tuned' in conceptually to her interests, provided appropriate resources, offered conceptual as well as associative language (Athey 2007) and were active participants in her play. Our close relationship continues, and the pleasure in being together and learning together is very special and highly valued by us as grandparents (Trevarthen 2002).

7 Last but not least was our commitment to **observe and record** Gabby's development and learning over such a long period of time. I have to say that, for me, it just became part of my routine. It was a pleasure to:

- notice and film or photograph anything that Gabby became engaged with at a deep level, or that gave her pleasure when we were together
- note down what she had done and said as accurately and near to the time as was possible
- chat with her mother each day and share with her where we had been and what we had been doing that morning.

The observation method of diarizing Gabby's words and actions meant that I have been able to include numerous quotes from the written diaries I kept throughout this book. Like Susan Isaacs almost 100 years ago, I wrote down in clear language, without making judgements initially, what Gabby had said (including gesture) and done each day. I used a 'grounded theory' approach when analysing the material I had gathered. Miller points out that 'the grounded theory approach is to move continuously from data to theory and back again' (2000: 118). The theory or concepts arise from the data and are validated, in this instance, by what happens next. Concepts or themes are coded initially in order to discover whether they occur more frequently than minor themes. To deal with the huge amount of data, I had to go through the diaries several times, marking up or coding anything that seemed significant or that linked with other observations. In some cases, I reduced the data to a table containing many observations with dates and ages so that I could easily look across the whole body of information and make links. I am attaching an example in the appendix.

For me, writing this book was a labour of love.

Appendix

From 1 to 2 Years – Gesture, Expressive and Receptive Language

Key

Ge = gesture
U = understanding
AID = Adult/Infant Drop-in
GT = Growing Together group
w = with
G = Gabby
N = Nicole
E = Evita
P = Paul

Age	Brief Description of Data
12m 3d	Maori music – very excited
12m 7d	Says 'more' and means it / Jigging as I walk towards CD player
12m 14d	Excited by music
12m 20d	Excited by music (Maori)
12m 22d	Put on 'Mamma Mia' – cries, dances, claps, bangs legs on floor
12m 29d	Looks at two books, takes G and N names off / Looks at felt book, puts name on it
13m 6d	N poorly, me telling stories G listens / Mirrors N's actions of talking then draws / Listens to 17 tunes on N's player and claps

Age	Brief Description of Data
13m 8d	Mum rings – puts phone to ear – smiles then looks at phone / Repeats 'ra ra' / Cries at GT when someone splashes her face
13m 11d	Can nod as well as shake head / Shrieks at 'round and round the garden' / Earlier, initiates rhyme by saying 'ra ra' and pointing Ge
13m 15d	Looks at The Baby's Catalogue then at own book
13m 29d	Says 'Mummummum' at bottom of stairs / When Paul reporting says 'Dadadad'
14m 17d	Calls water wheel 'Ra ra'
14m 22d	Very loud crying when cannot get on swing
14m 23d	Asks for music by pointing / Marches around waving at Jingle Bells / Looks at books / Says 'Bye bye' to nappy going in bin / Waves goodbye to staff Ge
14m 26d	I say 'asleep' – she feigns sleep Ge / In car saying 'Bar bar bar' and 'Dadada' / Understanding Paul and me U
14m 30d	I mention 'Baby Annabelle' U
15m	In car saying 'Yeh yeh yeh'
15m 1d	Talking to self in mirror / Loves Beach Boys CD – danced
15m 6d	Out for walk – responds to each dog and bird we pass / Stacks beakers – asks me to do it again / Me: 'Shall we get your dinner?' U
15m 8d	Paul reports her understanding / Communication / Recognizes word 'music' U
15m 12d	Enjoys singing / Teddy dancing to Beach Boys / Interested in 'ra ras'
15m 15d	At Rushden Children's Centre: cheeky grin and babble
15m 19d	Requests In the Night Garden
15m 20d	Bubbles / Jumps up and down and squeals with excitement
15m 21d	Asks for bubbles

(continued)

(continued)

Age	Brief Description of Data
15m 28d	Dances with two teddies and doll / 'Feeds' dolly, making movement and sound with her mouth
16m 3d	Says 'Pah' x5 when I refer to Pop / Her version of names when looking at family book 'Ga, Mumm, Dadadad, Gogo' / Gets teddy's trousers U
16m 4d	Following instructions U
16m 18d	Story *I Want My Mum* / Pointing Ge
16m 24d	MOVING most upset when music centre is packed
16m 25d	MOVING DAY Family Reading / music centre in new house
16m 27d	Looks at *I Want My Mum* for a long time
16m 30d	Very friendly in Mazza restaurant
17m	Likes singing, touches toes after 'Head, shoulders. . .'/ Most interested in story *I Want My Mum* – mirrors story / Plays shops w N talking to customers using microphone
17m 1d	Makes sounds after each mark / Listens to *I Want My Mum* for a long time
17m 7d	*I Want My Mum* – very interested in story
17m 10d	*The Very Hungry Caterpillar*: points at each item of food
17m 15d	At Colette's: story *I Want My Mum* / At Pen Green responds to 'Shall we go to soft room?' U
17m 18d	Meeting at PG looks at *I Want My Mum*
17m 23d	To theatre to see *We're Going on a Bear Hunt*: almost tells story Ge and U
17m 24d	Shows *I Want My Mum* to Pop and then me / Pop shows her a bird on phone that echoes speech – loves it
17m 25d	Cries loudly when I try to put borrowed top on her
17m 28d	New boots – very pleased – stamps feet / Walks through leaves
17m 29d	Looks at books / Pleased to open and close base of dish, almost cheering

Age	Brief Description of Data
18m 5d	Looks at books – rejects new baby animal book in favour of *The Baby's Catalogue* mostly + *The Tiger Who Came to Tea*, Nicole's book and *I Want My Mum* – looks at *I Want My Mum* with me and then Pop / Plays w 3D noughts and crosses and starts saying 'Ma!' each time she drops one into the box
18m 21d	West Glebe Park: shrieks with delight at large rotating swing
18m 26d	Practises frowning and other facial expressions / Loves 'zubberts' (noisy kisses) /Listens to story at school
18m 29d	Transports beads / Holds up finger for 'one more'
19m 2d	Defers gratification due to U
19m 4d	At PG sings 'Head, shoulders', 'Row your boat' – loves parachute – squeals with laughter / 'Soft room?' nods U
19m 10d	INTENT Buy small buggy and baby
19m 16d	Looks at *The Baby's Catalogue*, points, vocalizes / Uses gesture / Shows understanding U
19m 18d	Singing at PG w me and Paul – joins in w actions / Kisses Fiona (worker) goodbye / Frowns and shakes head in soft room when other children use steps / Plays w Pop's iPad repeatedly playing film of 'iguana at swimming pool in Florida' (filmed by Pop when we were on holiday) – points and makes sounds
19m 20d	Wicksteed Park: gestures up/down while pointing at trampoline Ge
19m 21d	At E&P's for dinner: practises facial expressions and bodily gesture / Head down, two hands on face and shakes head when we say we are leaving Ge
19m 23d	Will not say goodbye to N at school – shakes head / Oakley Vale Centre: enjoys singing and joins in with actions
19m 24d	Gives Colette a kiss / At Family Reading boy tickles her – she giggles / Finds specks of dust at home and says 'Er, er, er'

(continued)

(continued)

Age	Brief Description of Data
20m 1d	At meeting – looks at stories *The Tiger Who Came to Tea* and *I Want My Mum* and homemade book / At mine greets Pop with a kiss when he comes home
20m 2d	Holds a magnetic letter – I tell her 'a', she repeats / Understands two instructions U
20m 7d	Points to my bed – wants action rhyme 'One little monkey. . .'
20m 8d	East Carlton Park: wiggles her bum when ducks shake water off their bodies
20m 12d	Paul says G speaks to him on the phone for the first time today – babytalk but says 'Chow' – wants phone back when her mum is on it
20m 16d	Plays jumping on bed – points at 'The Kiss' by Klimt / Shrieks with laughter when Pop chases her / Looks at Little Princess book / Refuses to go on potty but points at Winnie the Pooh Ge
20m 27d	Oakley Vale Centre: mostly enjoys songs and rhymes – in car re-enacts, also looks at rhyme book, points at spider and I sing 'Incy Wincy. . .'/ At mine makes comparisons pointing at Pop's watch, mine and then old watch on her hand / Previously points at photo of Opi's glasses and then at mine / Looks at photos in hall with Pop Lots of Ge
21m	Comes to ours with Paul – looks at new photos in hall
21m 1d	Not herself / Frowns and makes noises when other chn come near in soft room Ge
21m 2d	Infant drop in – beckons me with a whole arm sweeping movement Ge
21m 6d	At their house – really likes story *The Very Hungry Caterpillar* – takes it in car – looks at it and makes sounds
21m 7d	West Glebe Park: chuffed dance after up steps and down slide
21m 16d	Parents off for a few days – I visit – G comes straight to me and lays her head on my chest for over 10 mins Ge

Age	Brief Description of Data
21m 21d	At hers: asks for music and dances round and round
21m 24d	To GT with me and Paul – much more settled – throws dough forward and behind then small amounts of sand, making a sound each time she throws it / Shrieks with laughter as she tries to catch bubbles and stand on them
21m 29d	Drop in group – new steps and slide – CHUFFLE (shuffle of chuffedness) Ge
22m 4d	Adult Infant Drop-in: makes a protesting sound when younger children approach
22m 5d	Drop-in group: Shakes head to all activities but nods head to soft room Ge / N says G cries when N goes w Tata (Nicole's father) / Also G kissed Tata when N did
22d 14d	GT uses rotating sharpener w Cessie – cries when finished U of explanation – evidence of thinking
22m 17d	West Glebe Park: interest in birds says 'Bir' / One finger up to signify 'one more turn' or 'again' Ge
22m 20d	Puts N's pj bottoms on – v pleased Ge
22m 26d	Town – shakes head to library? Shops? Nods to Costa / Afterwards nods to library – likes 'Incy Wincy' and does actions x3, likes a story called *Nat-tastic* about a boy who sneezes and becomes a superboy / At mine throws balls one at a time making a sound each time (like counting)
22m 27d	At ours – points to outside / Masters going up deep step – shrieks with pleasure / Keeps saying 'Bir' / I tell Pop about G trying on N's sparkly trainers and stamping feet – G understands and demonstrates / New word 'Peppa' also 'Kaka' / Replies to mum's Latvian with an emphatic 'Ja!'
23m 2d	CHICKEN POX: books *Where Do Baby Animals Come From?*, N's book and *The Baby's Catalogue* – has favourite bits – gestures baby playing peep-bo / 3D noughts and crosses – chants as she moves each one/ six plastic golf balls – throws them saying 'Ga' each time / Transports beads to table, saying 'Ma' each time – holds up one finger Ge

(continued)

(*continued*)

Age	Brief Description of Data
23m 5d	Bubbles in garden – says 'Bubba'
23m 10d	As we drive home, points at park Ge
23m 11d	GT At doll's house – gestures that something is missing Ge
23m 12d	Points at little park but too wet – cries / GT says 'Ra ra' at water wheel
23m 13d	Looks at *The Baby's Catalogue*
23m 22d	Puts beads on table and makes sounds as though counting / Stamps on bubbles and says 'Pop' / Pleased w self when carrying bottle and blowing bubbles
23m 24d	N shows her magnetic parts in kitchen 'Raises arms and laughs' v satisfied / Clonks herself on head w spoon when feeding baby – repeats it for fun Ge
23m 30d	West Glebe: cries when we leave

References

Arnold, C. (1997) Understanding young children and their contexts for learning and development: building on early experience. Unpublished Master of Education study, Leicester University.

Arnold, C. (1999) *Child Development and Learning 2–5 years: Georgia's Story*. London: Hodder & Stoughton.

Arnold, C. (2003) *Observing Harry: Child Development and Learning 0–5*. Maidenhead: Open University Press.

Arnold, C. (2007) Young children's representations of emotions and attachment in their spontaneous patterns of behaviour: an exploration of a researcher's understanding. PhD, Coventry University.

Arnold, C. (2009) Understanding 'together and apart': a case study of Edward's explorations at nursery, *Early Years*, 29(2): 119–130.

Arnold, C. and the Pen Green Team (2010) *Understanding Schemas and Emotion in Early Childhood*. London: Sage.

Arnold, C. (2014) Schemas: a way into a child's world, *Early Child Development and Care*, DOI: 10.1080/03004430.2014.952634

Arnold, C. (2015) *Doing Your Child Observation Case Study: A Step by Step Guide*. Maidenhead: Open University Press.

Arnold, C., Duffy, M. and Coe, S. (2018) The role of the family worker, in T. Gallagher and C. Arnold (2018) *Working with Children Aged 0–3 and Their Families*. Oxon: Routledge.

Asmussen, K. (2019) How parents support young children's understanding of things, people, numbers and words, *Early Education*, July 2019: 2–7.

Atherton, F. and Nutbrown, C. (2013) *Understanding Schemas and Young Children from Birth to Three*. London: Sage.

Atherton, F. and Nutbrown, C. (2016) Schematic pedagogy: supporting one child's learning at home and in a group, *International Journal of Early Years Education*, 24(1): 63–79.

Athey, C. (1990) *Extending Thought in Young Children*. London: Sage.

Athey, C. (2004–2005) personal communication.

Athey, C. (2007) *Extending Thought in Young Children*, 2nd edn. London: Sage.

Athey, C. (2013) Beginning with the theory about schemas, in K. Mairs and the Pen Green Team (C. Arnold (ed.)) *Young Children Learning Through Schemas*. London: Routledge.

Bion, W. (1962) *Learning from Experience*. London: Heinemann.

Blackburn, C. (2014) Policy-to-practice context to the delays and difficulties in the acquisition of speech, language and communication in the first five years. Thesis submitted as part of a doctorate, Birmingham City University.

Bowlby, J. (1997) *Attachment and Loss: Volume 1*. London: Pimlico.

Bowlby, J. (2005) *A Secure Base*. London: Routledge Classics.

Brazelton, T.B. and Sparrow, J.D. (2006) *Touchpoints 0–3: Your Child's Emotional and Behavioral Development*, 2nd edn. Cambridge M.A.: De Capo Press.

Brierley, J. and Nutbrown, C (2017) *Understanding Schematic Learning at Two*. London: Bloomsbury Academic.

Carr, M., Smith, A.B., Duncan, J., Jones, C., Lee, W. and Marshall, K. (2009) *Learning in the Making: Dispositions and Design in Early Education*. Rotterdam: Sense Publishers.

Cherry, K. (2020) Erik Erikson's stages of psychosocial development. Available at: www.verywellmind.com/erik-eriksons-stages-of-psychosocial-development (accessed 26 April 2020)

Cirelli, L.K., Trehub, S.E. and Trainor, L.J. (2018) Rhythm and melody as social signals for infants, *Annals of the New York Academy of Sciences*, 1423: 66–72.

Cole, C. and Gallagher, T. (2018) Growing together: a group for parents and carers with infants and toddlers, in T. Gallagher and C. Arnold (eds) *Working with Children Aged 0–3 and Their Families*. Oxon: Routledge.

Collins (2006) *Scrabble Dictionary*, Glasgow: Collins.

Cooper, H. (2002) *History in the Early Years*, 2nd edn. London: Routledge.

Côté-Lecaldare, M., Joussement, M. and Dufour, S. (2016) How to support toddlers' autonomy: a qualitative study with child care educators, *Early Education and Development*, 27(6): 822–40.

Csikszentmihalyi, M. (1992) *Flow: The Psychology of Happiness*. London: Random House.

Cvencek, D. and Meltzoff, A.N. (2015) Developing implicit social cognition in early childhood: methods, phenomena, prospects, in S. Robson and S. Flannery Quinn (eds) *The Routledge International Handbook of Young Children's Thinking and Understanding*. London: Routledge.

Delafield-Butt, J. (2018) The emotional and embodied nature of human understanding: Sharing narratives of meaning, in C. Trevarthen, J. Delafield-Butt and A-W. Dunlop (eds) *The Child's Curriculum*. Oxford: Oxford University Press.

Department for Education (2013) *The National Curriculum*. Crown Copyright.

Department for Education (2017) *Statutory Framework for the Early Years Foundation Stage*. Crown Copyright.

Department for Education (2020) *Development Matters: Non-Statutory Curriculum Guidance for the Early Years Foundation Stage*. Crown Copyright.

Donaldson, M. (1987) *Children's Minds*. London: Fontana Press.

Dunn, J. (1993) *Young Children's Close Relationships*. London: Sage.

Dunn, J. and Munn, P. (1987) Development of justifications in disputes with mother and children, *Developmental Psychology*, 23: 791–8.

Dweck, C.S. and Leggett, E.L. (1988) A social-cognitive approach to motivation and personality, *Psychological Review*, 95(2): 256–273.

England, L. (2018) *Schemas: A Practical Handbook*. London: Bloomsbury Publishing.

Ephgrave, A. (2018) *Planning in the Moment with Young Children*. London: Routledge.

Erskine, R. (2019) Child development in integrative psychotherapy: Erik Erikson's first three stages, *International Journal of Integrative Psychotherapy*, 10:11–34.

Faulkner, D. (1995) *Play, Self and the Social World*. Milton Keynes: Open University Press.

Fonagy, P., Luyten, P., Allison, E. and Campbell, C. (2018) Reconciling psychoanalytic ideas with attachment theory, in J. Cassidy and P.R. Shaver (eds) *Handbook of Attachment: Theory, Research and Clinical Applications*. New York: Guilford Press.

Fraiberg, S., Adelson, E. and Shapiro, V. (2003) Ghosts in the nursery: a psychoanalytic approach to the problems of impaired infant-mother relationships, in J. Raphael-Leff (ed.) *Parent-Infant Psychodynamics: Wild Things, Mirrors and Ghosts*. Oxon: Routledge.

Gelman, R. and Gallistel, C.R. (1986) *The Child's Understanding of Number*. London: Harvard University Press.

Gibson, J.J. (1986) *The Ecological Approach to Visual Perception*. Hove: Psychology Press.

Glasersfeld, E. von (1995) *Radical Constructivism: A Way of Knowing and Learning*. London: The Falmer Press.

Goldschmied, E. (1987) *Infants at Work* (video). London: National Children's Bureau.

Gopnik, A., Meltzoff, A. and Kuhl, P. (1999) *How Babies Think*. London: Weidenfeld and Nicolson.

Gopnik, A. (2009) *The Philosophical Baby*. London: The Bodley Head.

Grimmer, T. (2017) *Observing and Developing Schematic Behaviour in Young Children*. London: Jessica Kingsley Publishers.

Gruber, H.E. and Voneche, J.J. (1977) *The Essential Piaget*. New York: Basic Books.

Haylock, D. and Cockburn, A. (2013) *Understanding Mathematics for Young Children*, 4th edn. London: Sage.

Hornor, G. (2017) Resilience, *Journal of Pediatric Health Care*, 31(3): 384–390.

Isaacs, N. (1930) Appendix A: Children's 'why' questions, in S. Isaacs (ed.) *Intellectual Growth in Young Children*. London: Routledge and Kegan Paul.

Isaacs, S. (1952) The nature and function of phantasy, in J. Riviere (ed.) *Developments in Psychoanalysis*. London: Hogarth Press.

Jenvey, V.B. and Newton, E. (2015) The development of theory of mind, in S. Robson and S. Flannery Quinn (eds) *The Routledge International Handbook of Young Children's Thinking and Understanding*. London: Routledge.

Johnson, M. (2008) The meaning of the body, in W.F. Overton, U. Mueller and J.L. Newman (eds) *Developmental Perspectives on Embodiment and Consciousness*. London: Lawrence Erlbaum Associates.

Kettner, V.A. and Carpendale, J.I.M. (2013) Developing gestures for *no* and *yes*, *Gesture*, 13(2): 193–209.

Kuhl, P. (2010) Brain mechanisms in early language acquisition, *Neuron*, 67(5): 713–727.

Laevers, F. (1997) *A Process-Oriented Child Follow-Up System for Young Children*. Leuven University, Belgium: Centre for Experiential Education.

Laevers, F. and Declercq, B. (2018) How well-being and involvement fit into the commitment to children's rights, *European Journal of Education, Research, Development and Policy*, 53(3): 325–335.

Laevers, F. in collaboration with Daems, M., De Bruyckere, G., Declerq, B. et al. (ed.) (2005) *Well-being and Involvement in Care: A Process-Oriented Self-Evaluation Instrument for Care Settings*, Leuven: Research Centre for Experiential Education. Available at: https://www.kindengezin.be/img/sics-ziko-manual.pdf

Lake, G. and Evangelou, M. (2019) Let's Talk! An interactive intervention to support children's language development, *European Early Childhood Research Journal*, 27(2): 221–240.

Malloch, S. and Trevarthen, C. (2009) *Communicative Musicality: Exploring the Basis of Human Companionship*. Oxford: Oxford University Press.

Matthews, J. (2003) *Drawing and Painting: Children and Visual Representation*, 2nd edn. London: Paul Chapman.

Mendes, D.M.L.F. and Seidl-de-Moura, M.L. (2014) Different kinds of infants' smiles in the first six months and contingency to maternal affective behavior, *The Spanish Journal of Psychology*, 17: E80.

Miller, R.L. (2000) *Researching Life Stories and Family Histories*. London: Sage.

Nelson, K. (1986) *Event Knowledge: Structure and Function in Development*. Hillsdale, N.J.: Lawrence Erlbaum Associates.

Ofsted (2018) An investigation into how to assess the quality of education through curriculum intent, implementation and impact. Available at: https://assets.publishing.service.gov.uk/government/uploads/system/uploads/attachment_data/file/766252/How_to_assess_intent_and_implementation_of_curriculum_191218.pdf (accessed 26 October 2020).

Oh, J. and Lee, K. (2019) Who is a friend? Voices of young immigrant children, *European Early Childhood Education Research Journal*, 27(5): 647–661.

Oswell, D. (2013) *The Agency of Children: From Family to Global Human Rights*. Cambridge: Cambridge University Press.

Peters, S. and Davis, K. (2015) Babies, boys, boats and beyond, in S. Robson and S. Flannery Quinn (eds) *The Routledge International Handbook of Young Children's Thinking and Understanding*. London: Routledge.

Piaget, J. (1980) *Six Psychological Studies*, D. Elkind (ed.). Brighton: Harvester Press.

Rutter, M. (2013) Annual research review: resilience – clinical implications, *Journal of Child Psychology and Psychiatry*, 54(4): 474–487.

Shaw, J. (2019) A psychoanalytic framework for interpreting young child observations that integrates emotional and cognitive development, *Early Child Development and Care*. Available at: www.tandfonline.com/doi/abs/10.1080/03004430.2019.1698560 (accessed 26 October 2020).

Spence, K. and Clapton, G. (2018) Gender balance in the childcare workforce: Why having more men in childcare is important, in C. Trevarthen,

J. Delafield-Butt and A-W Dunlop (eds) *The Child's Curriculum*. Oxford: Oxford University Press.

Tait, C. (2005) Chuffedness as a measure of quality in an early childhood setting?, unpublished talk presented at the EECERA Conference, Dublin.

Thelen, E. (2008) Grounded in the world: developmental origins of the embodied mind, in W.F. Overton, U. Mueller and J.L. Newman (eds) *Developmental Perspectives on Embodiment and Consciousness*. London: Lawrence Erlbaum Associates.

Trevarthen, C. (2002) Learning in companionship, *Education in the North: The Journal of Scottish Education*, 10: 16–25.

Trevarthen, C., Delafield-Butt, J. and Dunlop, A-W. (eds) (2018a) *The Child's Curriculum*. Oxford: Oxford University Press.

Trevarthen, C., Delafield-Butt, J. and Dunlop, A-W. (2018b) The spirit of the child inspires learning in the community: How can we balance this promise with the politics and practice of education?, in C. Trevarthen, J. Delafield-Butt and A-W. Dunlop (eds) *The Child's Curriculum*. Oxford: Oxford University Press.

Vygotsky, L.S. (1978) *Mind in Society*. London: Harvard University Press.

Vygotsky, L.S. (1986) *Thought and Language*. Cambridge, MA: MIT Press.

Whalley, M. and the Pen Green Team (2017) *Involving Parents in Their Children's Learning: A Knowledge-Sharing Approach*, 3rd edn. London: Sage.

Winnicott, D.W. (1975) *Through Pediatrics to Psychoanalysis*. London: Hogarth Press.

Books for Children

Ahlberg, J. and A. (2012) *The Baby's* Catalogue (30th Anniversary Edition). London: Puffin Books.

Carle, E. (2002) *The Very Hungry Caterpillar*. London: Puffin Books.

Dodd, L. (2002) *Hairy Maclary*. London: Puffin Books.

Dodd, L. (2003) *Scarface Claw*. London: Puffin Books.

Dodd, L. (2014) *Slinki Malinki, Early Bird*. London: Puffin Books.

Edwards, D. (2010) *My Naughty Little Sister Stories*. London: Egmont.

Donaldson, J. and Kirtley, C. (2008) *Miss! Miss!* Oxford Reading Tree Songbirds Phonics, Level 2. Oxford: Oxford University Press.

Kerr, J. (2006) *The Tiger Who Came to Tea*. London: HarperCollins.

Milbourne, A. and Riglietti, S. (2012) *Where Do Baby Animals Come From?* London: Usborne Publishing.

Rosen, M. and Oxenbury, H. (2014) *We're Going on a Bear Hunt* (25th Anniversary Edition). London: Walker Books.

Ross, T. (2006) *I Want My Mum*. London: HarperCollins.

Snicket, L. and Klassen, J. (2014) *The Dark*. London: Orchard Books.

Walliams, D. and Blake, Q. (2010) *Mr. Stink*. London: HarperCollins.

Index

Page numbers in italics are pics.